Love & Language

Fiction
The Disappearance
*The One-Handed Pianist
and Other Stories*

Nonfiction
The Riddle of Cantinflas
Dictionary Days
On Borrowed Words
Spanglish
The Hispanic Condition
Art and Anger
The Inveterate Dreamer
Octavio Paz: A Meditation
Imagining Columbus
Bandido
¡Lotería! (with Teresa Villegas)

Anthologies
Lengua Fresca
(with Harold Augenbraum)
Tropical Synagogues
*The Schocken Book of Modern Se-
phardic Literature*
Wáchale!
The Scroll and the Cross
The Oxford Book of Jewish Stories
Mutual Impressions

*The Oxford Book of Latin Ameri-
can Essays*
Growing Up Latino
(with Harold Augenbraum)

Cartoons
Latino USA
(with Lalo López Alcaráz)

Translations
Sentimental Songs,
by Felipe Alfau

Editions
The Poetry of Pablo Neruda
Encyclopedia Latina (4 volumes)
*The Collected Stories of
Calvert Casey*
Rubén Darío: Selected Writings
*Isaac Bashevis Singer: Collected
Stories* (3 volumes)

General
The Essential Ilan Stavans
*Ilan Stavans: Eight Conversa-
tions*
(with Neal Sokol)
Collins Q&A
Conversations with Ilan Stavans

Love & Language

Ilan Stavans
WITH *Verónica Albin*

Yale University Press
New Haven and London

Designed by Sonia Shannon.
Set in Bulmer type by Integrated Publishing Solutions.
Printed in the United States of America.
Library of Congress Cataloging-in-Publication Data
Stavans, Ilan.
Love and language / Ilan Stavans with Verónica Albin.
p. cm.
Includes index.
ISBN 978-0-300-11805-6 (cloth : alk. paper)
1. Love.   2. Love in literature.   I. Albin,
Verónica, 1955–   II. Title.
BD436.S75 2007
128'.46—dc22
2007010478
A catalogue record for this book is available
from the British Library.

The paper in this book meets the guidelines for
permanence and durability of the Committee
on Production Guidelines for Book
Longevity of the Council on Library Resources.

10 9 8 7 6 5 4 3 2 1

The rest is silence.

—Hamlet, 5.2.358

CONTENTS

In 2002 Ilan Stavans caused an international uproar with the publi-
cation—in the Barcelona newspaper *La Vanguardia*—of his translation into Spanglish of part 1, chapter 1, of Miguel de Cervantes's
Don Quixote of La Mancha. A scrutiny of the debate that ensued
revealed the opposing sides: the foes, linguistic purists and pre-
scriptivists who fear that Spanglish heralds the ruin of the Spanish
language in the United States, and the endorsers, who believe that
the sizable Latino population north of the Rio Grande is a new
mestizo civilization in the making. The foes called Stavans an agent
provocateur who had stepped beyond his own scholarly boundaries, and they posited that a philologist should explore the transformations a language undergoes in history without attempting to
accelerate those changes. Those who endorsed Stavans's work
commended his bridging the gap between knowledge and action.

Among his foes, not unexpectedly, was the translation community in the United States, particularly those translators—including
me—who translate into Spanish for the U.S. market. When I read

that Stavans was delivering the Marilyn Gaddis Rose Lecture at the
American Translators Association's annual meeting in 2004, I decided to go listen to the enemy. For ninety minutes he contextual-
ized the mixing of English and Spanish by eloquently inviting the
audience to travel back in history to the colonial period in Latin
America and ponder the first encounter between *el castellano,* a
language described by the Salamanca scholar Antonio de Nebrija
as "compañera del imperio" (the companion of empire), and its
indigenous counterparts. He also reflected on Samuel Johnson
and Noah Webster, the origins and function of the Real Academia
Española, cyber-concoctions, and Hallmark greeting cards. There
was a delicious freshness and a sense of provocation to his approach. Enough to say that the enemy has become a treasured
friend and that I no longer see Spanglish, or language for that
matter, in the same light. Stavans is at once an incisive thinker and
a powerful storyteller.

Stavans grew up in Mexico City in the 1960s. His eccentric
and foreign-oriented home in the neighborhood of Copilco, in the
southern part of the capital, was home to immigrants who hailed
from Catherine the Great's Pale of Settlement. He spent his formative years in a Bundist school where instruction was imparted in
Yiddish. He learned Hebrew at Temple and Spanish in the neighborhood, and later studied other Romance languages. In 1985,
upon returning from a stint in Jerusalem, he left Mexico for the
United States and began honing his limited English skills with a
parting gift from his father—the third edition of *Appleton's New*

English–Spanish and Spanish–English Dictionary, edited by Arturo Cuyás.

The *San Francisco Chronicle* once described Stavans as a twenty-first-century Octavio Paz, approaching Hispanic culture as a vortex where a wide array of historical, social, economic, and religious forces coincide. Indeed, Stavans, the Lewis-Sebring Professor in Latin American and Latino Culture and the Five-College Fortieth Anniversary Professor at Amherst College, is a veritable cultural barometer. Although he belongs to an intellectual elite, he refuses to play the ivory-tower game and relishes getting his hands dirty. Equally comfortable and engaged at a library carrel reading Spinoza as on a bench in the *tianguis* reading *Memín Pinguín* or watching *Mucha lucha!* while devouring *unos buenos tacos,* Stavans can readily quote not only from history, literature, or Scripture but also from *telenovelas* and comic strips. He likes to remind people that in the sixteenth century Shakespeare's plays were seen as pop culture.

Stavans perceives the universe through words. The structure of his sentences might be said to be the structure of his thoughts. He's always probing into lexicographic definitions, delivering verbal puns, and calling attention to the differences between languages. It was our shared love for a very specific type of book—the dictionary—that connected us. In his book *Dictionary Days,* Stavans had vividly spoken of his love affair with words, so I approached him with the idea of embarking on an extensive interview on lexicography. Thus started our first collaboration, "On Dictionaries: A

Conversation with Ilan Stavans" for the *Translation Journal*. It was met with enthusiastic response. Collaborations on other topics— colonialism, libraries, and censorship, for instance—quickly followed. Some of the recurring themes in these conversations were translation, identity, and memory, about which Stavans has written eloquently in his autobiography, *On Borrowed Words*. Another topic that came to the fore repeatedly in our conversations was love in its various manifestations, including what Spinoza called *amor Dei intellectualis*.

I had just finished reading *Dictionary Days* and been particularly struck by chapter 7, "The Invention of Love," when I came across John R. Clarke's *Looking at Lovemaking: Constructions of Sexuality in Roman Art*. In it, Clarke argues that visual representations in ancient Rome are different from written text because they had a much wider and diverse audience and because the artists' values, unlike those of writers, were not necessarily those of the class they belonged to. The wide diffusion of sexual imagery in classical Rome as in our contemporary world opens up the possibility of seeing new faces and hearing new voices—those of people who have had no part in the literature of the elite. Therefore, in order to understand love, we must look at the visual record as well, but we must be careful not to do it through picture books. The elegant picture books have removed the sexual or erotic images from their original locations and taken them out of context. To gain an understanding of what love is and has been, we must attempt to contextualize it again.

When I talked about Clarke's views with Stavans, he observed that although phallic and other iconic or symbolic representations of genitalia or fertility are very common in many lands and periods in art, depictions of human sexual behavior are quite rare. They can be observed in only five traditions other than classical antiquity: pre-Columbian Peru, medieval India, ancient Egypt, and, closer to modern times, Japan and Western Europe. Could it be that sexual love, *amor veneris,* has been deemed less pressing than cooking, hunting, or warfare, and therefore less worthy of representation? Or is it seen as too important and so peppered with taboos as to prevent its representation in art? I wanted to find answers to these and other questions, and the one I wanted to take along on that journey was Ilan Stavans.

It was then that I proposed to him—and soon after to Mary Jane Peluso at Yale University Press—the possibility of embarking on a small volume on love. In spite of my curiosity, I must confess to initial trepidation. As soon as Stavans began probing the topic, though, making connections—patiently, melodiously, humanely, as is his style—and juxtaposing analyses, stories, and autobiography, my skepticism evaporated and Stavans's combination of warmth and bravura won me over. His passion for language, which I had first encountered in his understanding of Spanglish, is really a complex quest for meaning in a world saturated, maybe even anesthetized, by information.

Stavans approaches love as a series of concentric circles of attachment and also as an emotion defined by our architectural parameters. He talks of a person's travel from self-love to love of God and community; he also reconstructs the domestic space not as a romantic stage but rather as a place of struggle for status and identity, redrawing the lines between love and longing, nostalgia and loss. From the kitchen full of spices to the basement full of dread, Stavans, to paraphrase Gaston Bachelard, moves through the house exploring the hallways of human complexity, opening the doors of the psyche, the drawers of the imagination, and the cabinets of despair in search of that most amorphous human emotion.

Many societies—Acadian, Toltec, Viking, and Quechua, to name a few—don't even have a word for love. And when it comes to the English language, the monosyllabic word *love* has but inexact synonyms. In Stavans's view, there are five manifestations of love: self-love, erotic love, communal love, religious love, and love of country. In his engagement with me he touches upon all of them, but he pays special attention to the erotic, communal, and religious facets. In his discussion of Eros, he states that although dictionaries succinctly define morphemes for us, their precision is a façade. Love, he believes, is a most abstract emotion, understood differently depending on the coordinates of time and place. Each culture has a different approach to it.

In addition to visual representations, Stavans focuses on sexual behavior as portrayed in various literary genres, such as satire, elegy, comedy, mime, and farce. What piqued Stavans's interest in this area was that the terminology used to describe sexual behavior varies enormously across genres. He has a fondness for sarcasm (he constantly quotes from Ambrose Bierce's *The Devil's Dictionary*) but doesn't manipulate knowledge. He delves into the tradition of troubadour and courtesan poetry but prefers the Romantics, especially Samuel Taylor Coleridge. He also focuses on Shakespeare as the paragon of emotional explorations. He sees Sigmund Freud's psychoanalytic theories as charlatanry and finds more honesty and insight in Charles Darwin's *The Origin of Species.*

He talks about Plato's *Symposium* and about Leone Ebreo and Paolo Mantegazza, about Walter Benjamin and Roland Barthes. He's as passionate as he is eclectic. He alternates quotations with personal reflections—certainly not your typical academic response to a topic. Indeed, his mind tends toward the general and not the specific. He broadens rather than constrains. Surprisingly, his favorite genre appears to be not the essay but the poem, and he uses poems, which he often quotes from memory, to illustrate his points. These poems, when the lover's body is described, are riddled with clichés: the eyebrows are shaped like bows, the eyes shoot arrows that wound or kill, the teeth are pearly white, the mouth tastes of strawberries, the skin is smooth as silk (or velvet, take your pick), the cheeks are like peaches, and the object of desire is nameless and, in certain traditions, often depicted as a gazelle. Stavans is illuminating in his commentary on the biblical Song of Songs and also on the *Kama Sutra.* In chapter V, "A Catalog of Perversion," he explains how in the thirteenth century, for instance, the canonist Huguccio proclaimed that even within the sacrament of matrimony, even when sexual union occurred for procreation, the enjoyment of coupling was a sin. Stavans talks about venereal desire and some of its consequences, and how the delight in carnal pleasures led to lovesickness.

In terms of visual art, sometimes the topics we explore are due to serendipity, as when we stumbled upon a fabulous retrospective on Egon Schiele at the Neue Gallerie in New York, or when he found some pornographic representations of Walt Disney characters, but most often our exchanges address works by artists from traditions he knows well, such as the Mexican political cartoonist José Guadalupe Posada, the Spanish master Diego Velázquez, and scores of others from both the East and West.

The tête-à-tête that follows was conducted over twenty months during hours of formal working sessions, but it also took shape through idle walks in different cities, shopping sprees in bookstores, dinners at home surrounded by family, over coffee and donuts in museum cafeterias, and even in the emergency room in a Houston hospital. When we couldn't talk face to face, we used e-mail, fax, phone, and old-fashioned snail mail to exchange views, books, and scholarly papers. Sometimes I e-mailed him a catalog of questions I composed after probing a wide array of sources. On other occasions I fired off a batch of queries after discussing some of Stavans's positions with friends, colleagues, and my own students at Rice University. After a meeting, I would send him a transcript, asking him to expand on a particular topic. The result is a conversational narrative, a kind of Socratic dialogue about the flare-ups of being.

Every time I engaged Stavans, the setting seemed to color his responses. Thus, this book is part memoir, part confessional, part dissertation, part meditation, and an overall wonderful portrait of the man and his interests. Love brings ecstasy with the same ease as it does sorrow; it sets the imagination free as much as it enslaves the soul. Stavans finds it significant that in mythology Eros is paired with Psyche just as often as he is paired with Thanatos.

The six chapters and epilogue in *Love and Language* are not meant to be read sequentially. In fact, it is best to delve into the pages that follow the way one savors a snifter of sumptuous cognac: sporadically, in a state of contentment and relaxation. Their central motif, an extension of that luminous eight-page chapter in *Dictionary Days,* is that our views on love have undergone a series of radical transformations in the twentieth century, so radical that a new word for it might be needed. In Stavans's hands, the discourse of love includes tales of passion and bonds, devotion and piety, affection and alliance, family and loyalty, and thus the struggles in nation and empire. He explores love by discussing not only the texts of Western civilization, including the Song of Songs and the *Symposium,* but also the *Kama Sutra* and many other non-Western works.

Gracias, first and foremost, to Ilan Stavans for allowing his mind to roam free. I've yet to find a wall he is unwilling to scale, and that enthusiasm is contagious. A word of gratitude to Mary Jane Peluso at Yale University Press, whose idea it was to shape this volume, and to our editor, Jessie Hunnicutt, for her guidance and suggestions.

Three colleagues whose support has been unremitting are Hugo Enríquez Torres, Eliezer Nowodworski, and Martín Felipe Yriart—in Mexico, Israel, and Spain, respectively. They patiently read the manuscript and offered their unconditional wisdom. We are most grateful for their insight.

There are a few other colleagues who helped us every time we asked, and we shamelessly asked often. I have to thank Cathy K. Bokor three times: first for pampering me in Poughkeepsie with her fabulous Chicken Paprikash on my freezing trek down from Amherst, second for giving me the recipe, and third for serving as our adviser in Hungarian, that most complex and interesting of languages. Gabe, her *media naranja* and editor of the *Translation Journal,* I must also thank three times—for his generous help with the ten languages he has mastered, for being my sturdy and reliable sounding board, and for having repeatedly received Stavans and me so warmly in the *TJ.* To our research assistant at Rice, Richard K. Morse: thanks for providing fresh angles, Ketch. And to Rose Mary Salum, whose support in the early stages of this dialogue in *Literal: Latin American Voices* fanned the fire: *como siempre, mujer, mil gracias.* Rachel S. Edelman helped secure permissions. Finally, our heartfelt thanks to Neal Sokol for the preparation of the index.

V.A.

Love & Language

I

VORTICES OF LOVE

VERÓNICA ALBIN: How should the word *love* be defined?

ILAN STAVANS: As a most amorphous human feeling, capable
of extremes: attraction and repulsion, exultation and misery,
life and death, Eros and Thanatos.

The definition is imperfect, however, perhaps more so than
for any other feeling. How does one define hatred? And envy?
In fact, think about the way Western civilization conceptual-
izes feeling, as the condition of being emotionally affected. But
at what point aren't we emotionally affected? And how many
feelings are there? Five, like the senses? Seven, like the days of
the week, or better yet, like the deadly sins? Try cataloging
them and you'll fall prey to confusion.

VA: Are feelings and emotions the same?

IS: They have become synonyms, yes, although this is something
of a cliché. A feeling, the dictionary states, is an emotional

1

state, a disposition. Conversely, an emotion is the part of the consciousness that involves feeling. In any case, I prefer the word *emotion*.

VA : Why?

IS : Maybe it's a reaction. In the Mexico of my salad days, the word *sentimiento,* feeling, had a New Age quality. I remember the expression "estar en contacto con los sentimientos," to be in touch with one's feelings.

VA : What is the nature of an emotion?

IS : Emotions aren't quantifiable; they aren't even verifiable. Yet they rule our life from beginning to end. They are messy, rowdy, and turbulent. While they might be predictable, their patterns depend on circumstance and temperament. We don't fall in love because we want to, nor do we befriend a person by simply pressing a button. These actions are directed by an internal force. Reason might seek to control them, set limits to them, but emotions are autonomous; they exist beyond reason.

VA : How many distinct emotions are there?

IS : Let me offer an alphabetical, albeit partial, list of these nebulous experiences: angst, anguish, attraction, bereavement, betrayal, compassion, disappointment, ecstasy, elation, envy, exultation, failure, glee, gratefulness, guilt, happiness, hatred, helplessness, inferiority, insecurity, ire, jealousy, keenness, kinkiness, kinship, loss, love, meanness, misery, nostalgia, obligation, obsession, outrage, panic, pride, qualm, queasiness, regret, remorse, repulsion, revulsion, sadness, shame, trust, unhappiness, vulnerability, withdrawal, xenophobia, yearning, and zealousness.

VA : What makes love different?

IS : The fact that its contradictions make each of us feel unique.

VA : Contradictions or not, we know when we are in love . . .

IS : Therein my point: we know we're in love but can't fully explain what that means. Words are an attempt to articulate the confines of the emotion, but they are only that, an attempt. Emotions are fluid, loose, abstract, and unclenching, whereas words like to be concrete and unchangeable and to attach themselves to recognizable items or events. When words do manage to pinpoint an emotional state, it's only because we perceive it within specific coordinates, in a particular time and space. In spite of what we're commonly taught from an early age, love isn't universal. Its basic premise might concern a large number of individuals, but only when they share a set of cultural referents; otherwise the parameters are off. Indeed, love is a rather peculiar aspect of human relations that are defined by institutions and have a sense of tradition. To the Yanomami of the Amazon jungle, in southern Venezuela and northern Brazil, the concept is absolutely alien. It's not that Yanomami parents and children don't bond, or that friendships aren't forged. It's just that those relationships aren't described with the kind of lexicon we Westerners use to refer to our senses of loyalty and commitment.

In a similar vein, it's crucial to keep in mind that our understanding of love is in constant flux and that history is nothing but a sideboard of possibilities. Who can prove that what Cleopatra felt for Antony is the same as what Heloise felt for

Abelard? For that matter, is it possible to be sure that there is some kind of symmetry between what lovers feel for each other? Are there differences between genders? Does Romeo love Juliet the same way Juliet loves Romeo? Would the play be different had it been written not by William Shakespeare but by his wife, Anne Hathaway, or by his sister? These questions might appear to be obnoxious, but they prove the limits of our concept of love. What is it, really? Is there a way to measure it? Might it be studied scientifically?

VA : You're a perspectivist.

IS : I am. Years ago, in an essay entitled "The Verbal Quest," I wrote about a TV documentary in which an ethnographer had taken a phonograph to Africa and played songs by Edith Piaf for the Pygmies. Their reaction to the French pop star singing about passionate—mostly desperate—love was one of fright. First, they were unable to fathom that a tool as peculiar as a phonograph might be able to produce noise. But no sooner did the Pygmies hear Piaf emote about the penuries of romance than they looked for shelter. It's a matter of perspective.

One of my favorite philosophers is Giambattista Vico, the eighteenth-century thinker who was for years a professor of rhetoric at the University of Naples. His book *Scienza Nuova* (The New Science), first published in 1725 and rewritten a number of times, reconfigured the concept of a homogenized history for all humankind. He believed in cycles that went from simpler to more complex forms of socialization and was sure that all nations went through them at their own pace.

Each nation had to overcome primitive "vices"—as he described them—to achieve more sophisticated levels of civilization. "Of ferocity, avarice, and ambition, the three vices which run throughout the human race," Vico argued, "legislation creates the military, merchant, and governing classes, and thus the strength, riches, and wisdom of commonwealths. Out of these three great vices, which could certainly destroy all mankind on the face of the earth, it makes civil happiness." In other words, each nation has its own history. This idea was ahead of its time, which explains why Vico remained unknown until the nineteenth century. He's the father of historical perspectivism.

Likewise, each civilization sees love differently. Love doesn't change merely from language to language and culture to culture. It undergoes changes across time, too. Our elastic understanding of it today isn't the same as the one espoused by Plato in the fourth century BCE. Nor is it like the courtly love of the Renaissance. Stendhal's approach to it is different from Proust's and Freud's.

VA: I shall return to the topic of vices later on. For now, might we say that each civilization goes through the same cycle?

IS: I'm not convinced. Vico was a humanist. He didn't want to leave anything to mere chance. At heart he believed in a universal experience that sooner or later shapes us all, thus his approach to cycles. Notice that the approach still defines our conventional views on economic development. The colonial nations in Africa and the Americas known as "underdeveloped" will, we assume, eventually reach the sophisticated levels of the more advanced nations in Europe and the United States. This assumption is based on the belief that all economic systems travel a similar road, albeit at their own speed. I'm unconvinced this is true. Besides, love isn't about progress. Is our way of loving better, more advanced, than the Egyptians' and the Romans'? And by advanced, I mean superior. Is our love superior?

It's important to consider the age of empire as a disseminator of values. Ours is a global world as a result of incessant colonial adventures. The travels of Benjamin of Tudela across Europe and to Asia and Africa, the encounter of Marco Polo with the Mongol ruler Kublai Khan, the scientific explorations of Alexander von Humboldt, even the journey to the moon, are about homogenization. As Western civilization reaches beyond its limits, it recognizes otherness elsewhere on the planet, but it eventually permeates those regions with a set of values. A process of cultural translation takes place. In a patient negotiation, the models used by the empire eventually are adopted—and adapted—by the colony. The British colonization of India took place not only in the public sphere but also on a deeper level, affecting concepts like love and friendship, which over the years have become Westernized. The views on love in the Bible and those in the Mahabharata, one of the two major Sanskrit epics of ancient India, are different.

VA : As immigrants settle in another habitat, do their schemata regarding love change?

I S : That's a sharp question. Alison, my wife, would probably say yes, but I'm not sure myself. When I was a teenager, I used to love *a la mexicana.* I've become an American, though. Am I less effusive, more constrained? Maybe so. An immigrant's journey isn't qualified in geographical terms, the miles traveled. Instead, it's about inner transformations. How have you changed since you left the place of origin? In my own case, when I moved to the United States in 1985, I began a slow yet dramatic process of acculturation. Are there traces of the Ilan Stavans who left Mexico? If so, are those traces still reachable? Do I love nowadays *a la gringa?*

V A : Did Mexican Jews have their own style of love?

I S : Mimesis is a feature of Jewish life. As soon as Jews figure out the patterns of a new environment, they quickly incorporate those patterns into their natural behavior. In order to prove themselves authentic, they parade those patterns in ways only an outsider might. Eventually they become so confident that they actually start suggesting new patterns for the environment to adopt. Yiddish-speaking immigrants from the Pale of Settlement to Mexico loved the only way they knew how—the European way. Their descendants negotiated a change between the old ways and the new. In the past couple of decades, their grandchildren—the third generation—have been opening unforeseen vistas.

V A : When I studied Latin in Mexico, the verb *to love* was used to learn the first conjugation: *amo, amas, amat, amamus, amatis, amant . . .*

I s : The model was used not only when we studied Latin. Every
        dictionary of verbs in Spanish gives *amar* as the model for the
        first conjugation. For *-er* and *-ir* endings we are usually given
        two other verbs: *beber* and *vivir,* to drink and to live. Don't
        you find it ironic that they always use the same verbs? Maybe
        it's not ironic but symptomatic of a society like the Hispanic
        one, devoted to overemphasizing social conventions. The TV
        soaps might be proof that melodrama originated in Spanish
        comedias and operettas. Indeed, no matter how sober one
        might be, declarations of love often are melodramatic. Love in
        Western civilization is so frequently trivialized as to become
        histrionic.

v A : Where does the word *melodrama* come from?

I s : The *Oxford English Dictionary* offers an interesting definition.
        It states that in its early nineteenth-century use it was "a stage-
        play (usually romantic and sensational in plot and incident) in
        which songs were interspersed, and in which the action was
        accompanied by orchestral music appropriate for the situa-
        tions." It adds, "In later use the musical element gradually
        ceased to be an essential feature of the 'melodrama,' and the
        name now denotes a dramatic piece characterized by sensa-
        tional incidents and violent appeals to the emotions, but with a
        happy ending." It also defines the term as "a series of inci-
        dents, or a story true or fictitious, resembling what is repre-
        sented in melodrama." I quote from the 1971 edition. To me
        the *OED,* to use contemporary jargon, is "out of sync" with
        the world. The attribute *melodramatic* is described as "of or

pertaining to melodrama," that is, "having the characteristic of melodrama, often in a depreciative sense." But melodramatic is no longer a stage attribute. Instead, it's an essential component of day-to-day life. Our existences unfold in melodramatic ways when we express our emotions to others, be they love, hate, or other. The syrupy quality of romantic love and its ramifications—separation, revenge, reunion—have been defined to such an extent by the evasiveness of our concept of love that they automatically appear to us to be melodramatic.

VA : Doesn't your perspectivist view on love deprive the feeling of its charm?

IS : That kind of skepticism is rather old, don't you think? Does anyone still long for an immaculate view of the divine? Not until and unless we strip down the concept to its essence in an effort to understand its history and impact shall we be able to recognize the way it has shaped human endeavors.

Could you imagine life without love? My question isn't rhetorical; I'm honestly seeking to visualize a society where the concept doesn't exist. In fact, I suggest engaging in an exercise. Imagine for a second that love, the word we use to define so many different feelings, from kinship to sexual attraction to friendship, doesn't exist. Without love, much of who we are as a human community, I believe, would be radically different. The nuclear family, religious devotion, wisdom, sexual awakening, and marriage all rotate around the concept of love. Yet the Acadians didn't have a word for it. Nor did the Vikings. Before the Spaniards arrived in the so-called

New World, the Toltecs, Quechuas, Zapotecs, and other peoples functioned perfectly well without the need to have a word for it.

Jorge Luis Borges has a story I admire: "Averroës's Search." In it he describes the quest of Averroës, the twelfth-century Arab philosopher from al-Andalus (whose real name was Abu al-Walid Muhammad ibn Ahmad ibn Rushd), to translate Aristotle's *Poetics* into Arabic. When in the narrative Averroës, stationed in Cordoba, comes across the words *comedy* and *tragedy*, he faces a conundrum. What do they mean? He's at a loss, not because of personal ignorance—he is, after all, a learned man, author of the treatise *Tahafut-al-Tahafut* (Destruction of Destruction)—but because he has never seen a theater performance in his life. In Judaism and Islam, the prohibition against idolatry kept artistic manifestations like theater absent from culture. How then might Averroës describe the nature of a play if he doesn't even know what a stage is? At the end, according to Borges, he resorts to an absurd definition. I quote: "Aristu (Aristotle) gives the name of tragedy to panegyrics and that of comedy to satires and anathemas. Admirable tragedies and comedies abound in the pages of the Koran and in the *mohalacas* of the sanctuary." I should add that Borges's story is true. He found it in Ernest Renan's biography of Averroës, published in 1861. The Argentine even uses an epigraph from Renan: "S'imaginant que la tragédie n'est autre chose que l'art de louer . . ."

The same ought to be said about love. Can a people alien

to the concept experience it? Answer: only that which is understood actually exists. The limit of our knowledge is the limit of our experience. Indeed, our Western understanding of individual and collective freedom depends on the view we uphold: that a deep emotion shapes our attractions and repulsions, and that it's our duty to honor that emotion—within limits.

V A : In *Dictionary Days,* you devote an entire chapter to the word *love* in different languages: Russian, German, French, Italian, Spanish, English . . .

I S : I consulted a classic lexicon in each of those linguistic domains: Larousse in French, the *Diccionario de la lengua* of the Real Academia Española in Spanish, the *OED* in English, and so on. To my amazement, I discovered that each of these cultures approaches the feeling from a *slightly* different perspective. I emphasize *slightly* because even among Western cultures there are differences.

V A : Which do you prefer?

I S : Phonetically, I find *amor* in Spanish (a calque from the Latin *amor*) the most beautiful. It might have to do with my Mexican upbringing. The Romance languages play upon the same sounds: *l'amour, l'amore, o amor, l'amor,* and, the inspired Romanian variation, *iubire,* which shares an etymology with the English word *love.* In Medieval German it's *Lieb,* from the Latin *libens,* connected, as you might suspect, to *libido.* But I also like the word in Greek: *eros.* In any case, I learned about love, physically and emotionally, in Mexico. It's thus fitting that the language of Cervantes would hit closer to my heart. As L. Frank Baum states in *The Wizard of Oz,* "Hearts will never be practical until they can be made unbreakable."

VA : What about Yiddish?

IS : For me, the Yiddish noun *libe* (in German *Liebe)* is a term of endearment toward the community. My parents and grandparents partook of the culture of the Jews from the Pale of Settlement, a territory that corresponded to the historical borders of the Polish-Lithuanian Commonwealth and included much of present-day Belarus, Lithuania, Moldova, Poland, Ukraine, and parts of western Russia. The Pale, or "demarcation line"—Черта оседлости in Russian—was the result of a ukase issued by Catherine the Great in 1791 out of a nationalist and economic sentiment. In Russian society at the time the emerging middle class was rapidly being filled by an outcast stratum—the Jews. The Pale was created to restrict where Jews could reside so that a non-Jewish middle class could form. My upbringing in Mexico in the 1960s was defined by this culture and by a Bundist philosophy. The Bund—or, more precisely, the Yidisher Arbeter-Bund in Rusland, Lite, un Poyln—was a Jewish political party formed in Vilnius in 1897 that sought to bring all Jewish workers in the Russian Empire into a united socialist party. More important, it hoped to see the Jews achieve recognition as a nation with a legal minority status. The philosophy of this secular party was brought by Jews from the Pale to Mexico and elsewhere. For Bundists, the link between people depended on cultural empathy. The others, *los otros,* were often indicated as the depositories of selfless love.

VA: Could you delve into English-language definitions of love?

IS: In its 1971 edition, the *OED* devoted nine pages to the word and its variants. The first definition is cumbersome: "The disposition or state of feeling with regard to a person which (arising from recognition of attractive qualities, from instincts of natural relationship, or from sympathy) manifests itself in solicitude for the welfare of the object, and usually also in delight in his presence and desire for his approval." The *OED* almost never includes a parenthesis inside a definition. Couldn't the Oxford dons have done away with it? Happily, they kept it, for what is a parenthesis but an attempt to identify, to isolate, to insert, to emphasize, all of these strategies at the core of what love is about.

Samuel Johnson, more succinct, displays five definitions in his remarkable *A Dictionary of the English Language* (1755): (1) to regard with passionate affection, as that of one sex to the other; (2) to regard with the affection of a friend; (3) to regard with parental tenderness; (4) to be pleased with; and (5) to regard with reverent unwillingness to offend. Always generous in his quotations, Johnson includes, among other items, a segment from Shakespeare's *As You Like It* (5.2.82–83), when Phebe asks Silvius, "Good shepherd, tell this youth what 'tis to love." Silvius replies: "It is to be all made of sighs and tears."

Thereafter, as Johnson's quote continues, Silvius adds in line 89: "It is to be all made of faith and service." And then again in lines 93–97:

It is to be all made of fantasy,
All made of passion and all made of wishes,
All adoration, duty, and obedience,
All humbleness, all patience, all impatience,
All purity, all trial, all observance.

These obviously aren't references to *amor veneris,* though. It's the kinship of souls that's at stake.

VA: Why do you resort to Latin when speaking of love?

IS: Don't I sound more erudite than when I say carnal love? Spicing speech with foreign words is a sign of distinction. Latin appears to be dead, but in invoking it one communicates with the past. Or does one? (Joseph Solomon Delmedigo, the seventeenth-century Cretan physician and philosopher, believed that "if you judge by beards and girth, goats are the wisest creatures on earth.") Sprinkling a dialogue with French terms has a similar effect, although it evokes not erudition but romance. *Vous comprenez?* French, Italian, German, Latin—as long as the sound is foreign.

VA: And more pedantic. Let's stick to English. I Googled the word *love* one day and came up with 1,660,000,000 hits.

IS: More than a billion. In the language of the Internet, that amount is synonymous with infinity. As an expression, a billion nowadays has superseded a million. It used to be said, "I have a million chores to accomplish." A billion is a figure of speech, just as *The Thousand and One Nights* doesn't include 1,001 tales. In Arabic, the number 1,001 means any and all numbers together.

VA : As complex as we, and all those who have explored its nature, have discovered love to be, the English language seems to be most casual about it.

IS : In English, a genderless language, all one needs to worry about is having the guts to say "I love you." A man can say the three words, and a woman can say them too without any modifications. They are immutable. But in other languages, in other cultures, a declaration of love is most complicated. In one of the Arabic dialects, a man would say *uhebbuke* to a woman, but a woman would have to change the desinence to an *a* (*uhebbuka*) when addressing a man. The desinence would further change when used to address two men or two women (*uhebbukumaa*), or several men (*uhebbukum*). And some languages have two words that are the noun equivalents of *like* and *love.* Hungarian comes to mind: *szeretet* and *szerelem,* the latter being between a man and a woman (or between two men or two women) and always with sexual or romantic connotations. The structures of the verbs for these nouns are different: to like is *szeretni,* but to love is *szerelmes lenni valakibe* (to be in love with somebody). There's no simple verb for *szerelem; szerelmeskedni* means more or less "to play love games." *Szeretkezni* means "having sexual relations." The variations are almost infinite, since Hungarian can add a number of suffixes or prefixes to verbs to express different nuances. Interestingly, *szerelem* cannot be used to express love for *things,* be that chocolate or caviar. Spanish is also tricky, for not only does it have gender, but it makes a distinction between *querer* (to love) and *gustar* (to like sexually). And then there are the verbs *amar* (to love, perhaps more deeply than what is meant by *querer*) and *desear* (to desire).

VA : It seems that there's a typology of love in Western civilization.

I S : Let's start with zoology. Do animals love? In selecting a mate, a chimpanzee simply identifies a member of the opposite sex in order to copulate. It would be a stretch to describe this kind of choice as a sophisticated form of discrimination. Nevertheless, there's a preference exerted based on physical attraction. In that sense, biologists are right in reducing love to a chemical reaction. Yet it's important to proceed with caution. Maybe the most intriguing of all meditations on love is Charles Darwin's *The Origin of Species.* Its complete title is *On the Origin of Species by Means of Natural Selection, or the Preservation of Favoured Races in the Struggle for Life.* Published in 1859 and based on the research Darwin did during his voyage on the *Beagle,* it remains an astonishingly accessible scientific work, with a style that lay readers find engaging. In many ways, it's a love story of sorts, about the way living creatures mate and reproduce. That it established the theory of evolution is essential, but the volume is about much more than, as Darwin put it, "making one long argument." It's about attraction and repulsion, about origins and conclusions, about the survival of the fittest by what appears to be choice but in the end is part of a larger scheme of things. Ultimately, what Darwin, a nineteenth-century Victorian, forces on us is the recognition that no matter how free our mating decisions are, they conform to a set of rules where the weakest, unfavored link is likely to fall by the wayside.

VA : Is that love, though?

IS : Love per se isn't mentioned by Darwin, not explicitly. In his view, the interaction of organisms isn't about emotions but is about practical strategies for endurance. He discusses natural affinity and inheritance, and emphasizes strengthening aptitudes that result from crossbreeding. And how does Darwin explain beauty, for instance? He doesn't account for it. In fact, he dislikes anything connected with beauty. Species, in his eyes, don't evolve based on aesthetic principles. Furthermore, his isn't a theory of perception. Nonetheless, animal species, in Darwin's eyes, care about looks. An animal chooses its mate based on appearance. Think of a baboon's reddened buttocks, or a peacock's colorful feathers when they are fully extended. But that's because looks and functionality are linked. That is, there's a practical code in the DNA that moves animals to find a partner that will ensure the preservation of the species. At one point, Darwin does discuss this approach as aesthetic, announcing that "on the protest lately made by some naturalists, against the utilitarian doctrine that every detail of structure has been produced by the good of its possessor," a living organism in the animal kingdom behaves according to an aesthetic principle. This is what Darwin means by structure. It isn't aesthetics as humans understand them but the capacity to entice a member of the opposite sex by changing one's appearance. That change involves the enhancement—beautification?—of the mate's qualities. And the enhancement generates sexual excitement. Darwin adds about the naturalists: "They believe that very many structures have been created for beauty in the eyes of man, and for mere variety. This doctrine, if true, would be absolutely fatal to my theory. Yet I fully admit that many structures are of no direct use to their possessors."

VA : Love and pure attraction aren't the same, then.

IS : The nuances are such that it's difficult to distinguish between them. Surely they are interrelated. Attraction is about magnetism, an inner force compelling one object to be with another. Yet animals experience more than sheer attraction. There's loyalty in them and also an unadulterated form of love.

VA : Unadulterated?

IS : Plato's *Symposium,* arguably the most important—and maybe the oldest—treatise on love in Western civilization, written in the fourth century BCE, is modeled after a banquet, a "drinking together" (as the word *symposium* means in Greek) in honor of Eros. A practice in ancient Greece was to have a party in someone's house and, after the food and wine were served, allow the guests to deliver speeches while entertainers lightened the atmosphere. Plato has Socrates discuss in front of others the concept of love as "a desire for perpetual possession of the Good and Beautiful."

Socrates, of course, is Plato's mouthpiece. Much like Jesus Christ, he is an emblematic figure whose legacy depends on heresy. With Jesus, we have the four Gospels, written a posteriori by people unacquainted with him, as a record of his martyrdom. Likewise with Socrates. Among the surviving material we have a handful of Plato's dialogues; another handful of less-stylized ones composed in old age by Xenophon, whom I. F. Stone called "platitudinous and banal, sometimes a downright philistine"; some comments by Aristotle; and some plays by Aristophanes, chief among them *The Clouds,* although Socrates is also mentioned in *The Birds, The Frogs,* and *The Wasps.* Commenting on Socrates' trial was a sport among Athenians. But we don't have Socrates' words as a firsthand account. He was a free-thinking philosopher infatuated with the Spartan ways. He was also a rough, vain, and uncommitted man, whose words did not always match his deeds. Did he discuss love, among other topics, in the fashion that Plato suggests? Socrates isn't quite a subaltern, although he is, in my view, a puppet of sorts, a tragic hero of the intellect but not a man of even the most essential of emotions. Among Socrates' famous acts after the trial, which took place in 399 BCE, is one described in Plato's *Phaedo.* In the dialogue, just after the trial, Socrates' wife, Xanthippe, is next to her husband, along with some pupils who are plotting his escape. She has one of her sons in her arms.

Plato says, "Now when Xanthippe saw us, she cried out and said the kind of thing women always do say: 'Oh, Socrates, this is the last time now that your friends will speak to you or you to them.'" In a moment like this, one would expect Socrates to approach her, say a few caring words, and embrace her. Instead, he ignores her and ignores the child. Is this the way the promoter of "a desire for perpetual possession of the Good and Beautiful" expresses love and compassion to his own partner?

VA: Why was he tried?

IS: Ah, a crucial question. Everyone knows about Socrates' fate. But what was he guilty of? Xenophon says he was accused of teaching the Athenian youth to look down on the laws and to lead them "to despise the established constitution." This, Xenophon implies, made Socrates' followers violent. In other words, he was perceived to be seditious, opposing the status quo. The accusation, however, is peculiar if we consider that Athens, having gone through a tyrannical period, was a democracy that valued freedom of expression—it was a marketplace of ideas. So why would Socrates be accused of sedition and persecuted in a landscape where the speaking of one's mind was considered to be an asset?

I believe Socrates wanted to be a martyr. He recognized the limits of individual knowledge and the freedom embraced by Athenians. He had a chance to defend himself in the trial but instead chose to antagonize the jury. He also had an opportunity to avoid punishment when a number of his pupils plotted his escape, yet he rejected this exit. Like Jesus Christ, he needed an alibi to die. He was already past seventy, and old age was too penurious a stage for him. Some of his students used his teachings to advocate principles removed from Socrates' philosophy, while others not only remained loyal to him but even turned him into a saint. In short, his death was an act of self-immolation.

VA: Does that diminish his stature?

IS: Not in the least. To die the way one wishes is an art.

VA: Earlier, you questioned whether *The Symposium* is the oldest extant rumination on love. Is it?

IS: The intellectual foundation of Western civilization is Greek mythology. Bertrand Russell believed that every philosophical conundrum we're exposed to might be resolved using either Plato's tools or Aristotle's. The rest, as he put it, are footnotes. The Eurocentrism that defines us, well founded as it is, often eclipses other versions. How much do we know about other reflections on love produced by previous cultures?

In any case, the theory offered in *The Symposium* is that of the perfect union. Popular knowledge reduces it to finding the "other half"—as though one were speaking of an orange! Before birth there's completeness. But our arrival on earth represents the cutting in half of the soul, a division in two. Thus, throughout life our quest for love is based on the need to find the missing part of ourselves. Plato writes beautifully about a concept that would ultimately become the *union mystica:*

Each of us when separated, having one side only, like a flat fish, is but the indenture of a man, and he is always look-

ing for his other half. . . . And when one of them meets with his other half, the actual half of himself, whether he be a lover of youth or a lover of another sort, the pair is lost in an amazement of love and friendship and intimacy, and will not be out of the other's sight, as I may say, even for a moment: these are the people who pass their whole lives together; yet they could not explain what they desire of one another. For the intense yearning which each of them has towards the other does not appear to be the desire of the lover's intercourse, but of something else which the soul of either evidently desires and cannot tell, and of which she has only a dark and doubtful presentiment.

The theory explains love as an addition and subsumes yearning and desire to it. To find our other half isn't only to be complete again but to return to our origin. Shlomo ibn Gabirol, a Spanish-Hebrew poet of the eleventh century, believed that "love renders one blind and deaf."

For centuries Plato's theory justified the "oneness" of love. It makes reference to the sacredness and universality of love, which is at once unconscious and ingrained in the human soul. The soul for Plato is the essence of the self, what Carl Gustav Jung would later call the anima. Today it might also be taken as a synonym for individual character. The *OED* defines the word *soul* as "the principle of life in man and animals." Then it expands a bit: "The principle of thought and action in man, commonly regarded as an entity distinct from the body; the spiritual part of man in contrast with the purely physical." Modernity has turned us into skeptics, but philosophers have always debated the possibility of animals having souls, too. In *Phaedrus,* Plato talks of the soul as "something which moves itself," and in the *Laws* he repeats the concept: "a motion which moves itself." For him, the soul is a purposeful motor connected to reason.

Yet human love for Plato has different connotations, different vortices, I might say. He talks of a lover's love, a friend's love, a parent's love, a teacher's love, a leader's love. He also discusses spiritual forms: love for the divine, knowledge, and nature in all its aspects. In the Greek language there are different words for love that suggest nuances, and it isn't easy to distinguish between them. The word *eros* (ἔρως) is mostly taken to mean a type of love ruled by desire, a mix of passion and sexual urge. *Agapē* (ἀγάπη) denotes affection and concern and is used when describing the relationship between a teacher and a student. *Philia* (φιλία) means friendship, and *storge* (στοργή) affection.

There are myriad interpretations of love, like that of Leone Ebreo, a Spanish thinker (although he was actually born in Lisbon), doctor, and poet, whose book *Dialoghi di amore* was incredibly influential in the Renaissance. His full name was Judah Abrabanel. He was the son of Isaac Abrabanel, the biblical commentator, philosopher, and businessman who in 1492 tried, along with Abraham Senior, to convince King Ferdinand of Aragon to revoke the edict of expulsion of the Jews from Spain. In fact, he offered Ferdinand a large sum of money— some say 600,000 *maravedíes*—and, it appears, the monarch seriously considered the bribe. But in the end, so the rumor goes, the Grand Inquisitor Tomás de Torquemada, who may have been a convert from Judaism, talked him out of it by making an analogy to Judas's thirty pieces of silver. Leone Ebreo left Spain with his father when the exodus took place, and they moved to Naples. *Dialoghi di amore* was written in Italian in 1502 (some believe it was a decade earlier). It's shaped in the form of a Plato-like conversation—a typical device of the time, used by Judah Halevi in *The Kuzari,* and by many others—between fictional characters. The characters are Philone and Sophia, names with obvious etymological resonance. Plato's philosophy is the backbone of the entire argument, since Ebreo believes that the driving force and the constant in the world is love. His argument rotates around the concept of beauty, which for him is an essential component of love. The beauty of the universe, Ebreo argues, is part of a divine design. The human quest is to appreciate that beauty and to embrace it. The other concept behind Ebreo's thesis is moral good. To love the divine is to follow the moral code. He believes that the ultimate objective of humans is to embrace the divine through a union, and that such a union is essential to nature. He talks about "circles of love" as a way for nature, the divine, and the individual to become one and the same.

V A : Is that perfection?

I S : Indeed, Ebreo trusts that love brings perfection. It's an abstract love. In *Dialoghi di amore* there is no interest in sexual intercourse, which, it seems, is animal behavior. Humans, instead, must seek refinement of a spiritual kind. Love is about sublimation.

VA: The concept of "circles of love" is found frequently in popular culture.

IS: What basic geometric figure comes to mind when you think of love? Not the square. Maybe the triangle: a ménage à trois, a love triangle, the expression "three's a crowd," and so on. But the quintessential figure is the circle. Plato's two halves are in it. The circle is an emblem of completeness. But in creating a connection between God, nature, and people, Ebreo talks of concentric circles. In contemporary popular culture, one comes across images like an orange that needs to be peeled, an onion whose layers define various modalities of love, and the heart, which is depicted in plastic terms, its roundness highlighted. As for me, the vortices of human love are concentric: first comes self-love and then family love. Third comes romantic love, followed by love for a higher being, and finally the love of community. In Ebreo's *Dialoghi di amore,* there are influences of the *Guide of the Perplexed* by Maimonides, who was by far the most important Jewish philosopher and moralist of the Middle Ages. In turn, Ebreo influenced Spinoza, a rationalist who left some margin in his geometrical universe for emotions.

VA: How so?

IS: In his book *The Ethics,* Baruch Spinoza, the seventeenth-century Dutch thinker, compartmentalized knowledge geometrically. But he included not only intellectual data; he also categorized emotions. One of those emotions, according to him, is love.

I find Spinoza's life and thought immensely compelling, if also a defeat of human reason. Ostracized by the Jewish community for his heretical supposition that the divine *isn't* a single entity but is Nature itself, he attempted an impossible task: to explain every aspect of the world in intellectual terms and following a precise order, as he polished lenses. For Spinoza was also a patient student of optics, the discipline devoted to the study of sight. What do we see? How do we see it? In any case, he wasn't a cold, reticent person, as history often portrays him. On the contrary, he was passionate and engaged. For him love also meant a union of sorts with the divine. *Amor Dei intellectualis* is a manifestation of a person's desire to understand and know how the universe functions and to embrace God as its cause. It isn't an impervious or chaotic emotion, but one that is carefully calibrated. For Spinoza love comes from understanding and also awe at the wonders of creation: to appreciate the universe is to love it through the intellect.

v a : Spinoza views love as a combination of emotion and reason.

i s : Yes, and this combination is as old as humankind. For as much as we try to separate them, the mind and the heart dance together, don't you think?

v a : Spinoza strives for another type of perfection.

i s : Intellectual perfection. His mind might well have been the purest, the most methodical, to ever inhabit the earth. Even if untrue, the mythical portrait of him as distant, a hermit, one devoted to the sharpening of the mind without the miserable interruption of daily affairs, has charm. It makes me think of the first line in Francisco de Quevedo's memorable sonnet, "Alejado en la paz de estos desiertos, con pocos pero doctos libros juntos"—retired in these peaceful deserts, surrounded by few yet erudite books. Spinoza is seen as a predecessor of Melville's Bartleby, proudly claiming "I would prefer not to!" But again, this is sheer fiction. The Dutch philosopher wasn't a refusenik; he was a worshiper of reason as the ultimate force of civilization. In his weltanschauung reason expresses love. Haven't you felt something similar when you finally conquer a challenging topic? Not long ago I decided to study, line by line, scene by scene, Shakespeare's seven tragedies: *Romeo and Juliet, Julius Caesar, Hamlet, Othello, King Lear, Macbeth,* and *Antony and Cleopatra.* How are they structured? What kind of narrative economy do they sustain? How does Shakespeare build each individual character? Is there continuity between these plays? What is the view of human affairs depicted in them? And did Shakespeare—a mere mortal—manage alone to create such an extraordinary sequence, unrivaled anytime before or after? I committed myself to the task, spending a couple of months on it. In the end, did I answer my questions? Only partially. But that doesn't matter. What matters is the feeling of having an intellectual task to pursue. I came out of it *loving* Shakespeare above any other artist. In fact, I came out loving the idea that, through calibrated language, someone had managed—and I use one of Hamlet's images—to "hold a mirror up to nature."

V A : Are there any other major thinkers on love, in your view?

I S : There's Paolo Mantegazza, who wrote two books on pain and love at the end of the nineteenth century. He called his books on the topic *Fisiologia del dolore* and *Fisiologia del amore*. In the twentieth century, José Ortega y Gasset, Denis de Rougemont, Herbert Marcuse, Michel Foucault, Georges Bataille, and Octavio Paz wrote insightful meditations.

V A : You wrote about Paz in a small volume you published on him in 2001.

I S : In 1993, about to reach the age of eighty, Paz came out with a book-length essay called *The Double Flame*. I read it immediately. At the time I was still an ardent admirer of Paz, even though I had begun to question my opinions. Any new book by him was an occasion; I would run to the bookstore to buy it. When it was released in an English translation by Helen Lane in the United States a couple of years later, I reviewed it for the *Washington Post*. Paz is a cosmopolitan figure whose understanding of culture is defined by his Mexican upbringing.

V A : Somewhat like you.

I S : His style is lyrical and thought provoking. His main interest is in understanding the way humans transform sexuality into performance, much in the way that a sculpture transforms a stone into a work of art. In other words, Paz is interested in sexuality as ritual and, as such, in understanding the function of ritual in human life. *The Double Flame* surveys the history of love with one objective in mind: to understand the relationship—one he was concerned with since early on in his career, infatuated as he was with surrealism—between eroticism and poetry. Not too long ago I tried rereading it. It had been published more than a decade earlier (and there are parts Paz acknowledges having written decades before), yet it seemed to me that it still held up well. But I think that it doesn't have the zeitgeist of Foucault's three-volume *History of Sexuality,* an unbalanced yet pugnacious analysis of sexuality during Roman times and an indictment of the belief of sexual repression in Western civilization. The first volume, *The Will to Knowledge,* published in French in 1976, is by far the most focused. Foucault reflected on desire and its institutionalization in society in a provocative fashion. The problem is that deep inside he's a skeptic. I'm surely not the first one to say it. His nihilistic view of reason questions the importance of moral values. Yet at his core he depends on reason and even upholds it in his oeuvre. In brief, I see Foucault's propositions as a short-circuiting of ideas, never fully convincing in their foundations.

v a : What about Freud? He revolutionized our understanding of sexuality. I'm surprised you haven't mentioned him yet.

i s : But did Freud make us understand better the emotion we call love? On the contrary, through his pseudoscientific endeavors Freud took the sublime away from it. He reduced the attraction between two individuals to a mechanical sequence. Like Mantegazza, his early experiments were done using cocaine— he called it "the magical drug"—and hypnosis. One would think that, as a result, he would be less incisive. But he saw himself as a scientist, which is a major mistake if your purpose is to understand human emotions. His *Interpretation of Dreams* is obnoxiously simplistic: a set of sex-related symbols populate our unconscious, struggling to deliver their message to us while existing under the tyrannical control of the ego. A plane, a machete, and a banana are the penis, a tunnel and a fig are vaginas, a balloon and a jar are breasts, and so on. Ay, ay, ay . . . how naïve and one-dimensional! How crude to reduce the history of dreams to caricature through a set of easy-to-use codes! Dreams play an essential role in our love life. Yet nothing is more dangerous than offering counsel through them. The lover is imagined, even invented by us in endlessly creative ways. Some of these ways are defined by sexuality, but there's more—much more—in the act of love. "Learn from your dreams what you lack," W. H. Auden said in *The Sea and the Mirror.* My dreams are a fundamental component of my life. I cherish them, and while I'm often stymied from remembering them, I wouldn't want them reduced to sheer memos of my unconscious. To this Foucault was right in reacting . . . It would be better to lie, to invent dreams, which isn't at all difficult. In *Lolita,* Vladimir Nabokov includes a terrific passage. It comes to mind when thinking how reductive Freud is: "I discovered there was an endless source of robust enjoyment in trifling with psychiatrists: cunningly leading them on; never letting them see that you know all the tricks of the trade; inventing for them elaborate dreams, pure classics in style (which make them, the dream-extortionists, dream and wake up shrieking); teasing them with fake 'primal scenes'; and never allowing them the slightest glimpse of one's real sexual predicament."

VA: You see Freud as a fraud, but you wouldn't deny his influence.

IS: It's enormous, for sure. But the idea of mapping out the élan vital predates Freud. His age was defined by the scientific discovery, in the realm of physics, of energy in all its dimensions. Freud, a genius in the art of repackaging ideas, was influenced by this mapping in creating his hierarchical triptych: the superego, ego, and id. The ego is the battlefield where social conventions and natural impulses collide. This clash is an attempt to conceptualize love. It fails the test, though. Yes, love is energy. But it's also much more. Plus, as we discussed before, each collectivity defines love differently according to time, geography, and need.

I should say that Freud is one of the most mesmerizing scientific writers ever. His case studies are stories of hope and deceit, narrated with flair and command. Years ago, when I edited *The Oxford Book of Jewish Stories,* I tried convincing my in-house editor to include him. She turned the idea down.

VA: What piece did you select?

IS: The case of Anna O., the pseudonym he used for the epileptic patient Bertha Pappenheim, a Viennese Jew. Aside from her fame as Freud's and Josef Breuer's patient, she founded orphanages and organizations to promote Jewish women's contributions.

VA: Freud made popular the adjective *libidinous.*

IS: A synonym of *lustful.* The *OED* records *libido* as a "psychic drive or energy, particularly that associated with the sexual instinct, but also that inherent in other instinctive mental desires and drives." What is more, the Oxford dons define *libidinous* in a rather curious fashion: "Of persons, their lives, actions, desires." They add: "Given to, full of, or characterized by lust and lewdness." Freud, himself a rather "repressed" person, was obsessed with lust.

In the studies of love I've encountered over the years, my own favorite—although not a disquisition per se—is the oeuvre of the Marquis de Sade. The word *sadism* comes from it. And our contemporary understanding of lust, eroticism, and pleasure is framed by this creature of physical experimentation.

VA: I'd like to leave Sade for later conversation.

IS: My interest in him won't cease, I promise.

VA: Meanwhile, I want to test your conception of love in terms of concentric circles while at the same time using it as a surveyor's map. In other words, I'd like to organize our tête-à-tête in that order, from self-love to love of community.

IS: *Adelante.* I should add another dimension, however—one in connection with Foucault. In our culture, love is defined by loci. I frequently discover myself thinking of love in architectural ways. The love experienced in the bedroom is different from the love at the dinner table. Likewise, the love defined as forbidden is left for obscure, hidden places like the basement and the closet. In some ways, we could think of a house as a map to the way we approach love: the mirror, the bed, the boudoir, the desk . . .

VA : Let's try combining the two approaches, the one defined by degrees of attachment and the architectural one. Why does self-love come first in the typology?

IS : It's the first stage in our encounter with the universe. A baby is sheer instinct as well as absolute egotism. Nothing exists beyond thirst and hunger. The desire to be comforted becomes a condition. Throughout life, that egotism remains a driving force. And eroticism is reduced to self-satisfaction. We have yet to discover the pleasures of encounter. Only our body matters. As we grow up, we are taught that living among others means sharing.

VA : Freud defined self-love as narcissism.

IS : There's a painting by John William Waterhouse, the British pre-Raphaelite, entitled *Echo and Narcissus*. It's an emulation of Renaissance art done in 1903, which is suitable to explain Narcissus's symbolism. The young man, partially naked—he's covered by a red tunic—is lying facedown on a rock next to a pond in the middle of a forest, admiring his own image. Next to him is Echo, the beautiful nymph, in whose pond Narcissus finds himself. She, too, is scantily clothed (her left breast is exposed), facing us, with her head turned in Narcissus's direction. In the *Metamorphosis,* Ovid described Narcissus as being handsome to such a degree that he's caught in his own image, ignoring Echo's interest. He's eventually condemned to the fate of falling in love with his reflection. In psychology, a modicum of narcissism is acceptable; too much is seen as an illness. But narcissism and self-love aren't the same. In fact, we're talking apples and oranges. Self-love isn't about physical beauty, as the Greek myth is, but about appreciation of our internal image. The French call it *amour propre,* a synonym for self-respect. The transition from childhood to adulthood is a period of discovering worth, of recognizing the limits of the self. The realization that others aren't like us and that we're unique and different enables us to find a niche, to carve a place of our own, to understand our true worth. The domestic fitting that best represents this type of love is the mirror, not in the sense of obsession but in the sense of self-preservation and self-respect. When looking in the mirror, every single one of us is convinced of our own beauty. We learn to live in the body, to believe that it's the center of the universe. That drive also pushes us to protect ourselves, to *love* our efforts. Alexander Pope, in the second epistle of his "Essay on Man," states that "Self-love, the spring of motion, acts the soul." Thus, our self-perception becomes an engine, driving us to fight for independence. It's an effort shaped by our consciousness. As Pope suggests, "Self-love and Reason to one end aspire."

VA : In what sense is that love the same emotion we manifest to others later on?

IS : Self-love is also about dialogue, what the modernists described as "stream of consciousness." Each of us is menaced by a barrage of private mental communication. To keep that private verbal mode going is to be normal. To let it become public is not only indiscrete, it threatens our integrity and balance.

VA : Don't vanity and self-love go together?

IS : Vanity is the feeling of excessive pride, but it also might refer to the trait of being vain and conceited. We all shape our self-esteem through a moderate dose of vanity. And in love, that vanity plays an important role. The need to look attractive, clean, and well-dressed, to fit into the circumstance of the moment, gives place to pride. The piece of bedroom furniture, a low table with mirrors, where one sits while dressing or applying makeup is called a vanity.

The expression "to cover one's vanity" refers to the need to hide the sexual organs. Venus is the goddess of vanity. She's often depicted undressed, proudly displaying her body. Among the best paintings of her is Diego Velázquez's *La Venus del espejo,* made in 1644 (some art historians claim it was done in 1648). In it a fully naked Venus lies with her back to the viewer. She languishes on a bed of white linen with a black spread. Red draperies hang in the background. Venus looks at herself in a mirror held by a half-kneeling Cupid. We see her face reflected. This is the only existing painting by Velázquez of a naked woman. Who was she? There's little biographical information. It could be the painter's wife or perhaps his lover. Why don't we see her frontally? There's a slight element of indiscretion in her, as if she were caught in her vanity by the painter. Velázquez is shrewd enough to make the image on the mirror nebulous. The color of her flesh is unsullied, even exquisite, and contrasts sharply with the strong red, black, and white of the fabric that surrounds her. A reminiscence of

Rubens's women comes to mind: Venus isn't portly, but the shape of her torso, as a result of her reclining position, emphasizes her female lines. From the toes of her left foot to her prostrate right arm, there's a harmonious horizontal perspective in the painting, going from left to right.

VA : Is the position of the mirror in *La Venus del espejo* accurate?

IS : Only if we agree that, because of the angle, she's seeing not herself but the painter—or, as in the case of *Las meninas,* she's seeing us, the viewer. Therein lies the power of the painting, which has tantalized me for years: it's about vanity, insofar as vanity is understood as a conceit. It isn't that Venus is proud of her appearance; she's proud of the painter—the viewer—looking at her.

Velázquez assiduously used mirrors in his oeuvre. This isn't an accident. He comes toward the end of the so-called Spanish Golden Age, which produced a baroque art. And what is baroque? The style that constantly makes reference to itself, to the degree of becoming a caricature. Quevedo's *Sueños,* his pastiches on life and philosophy, are self-referential. Luis de Góngora didn't so much refer to himself as push his language to become self-conscious, giving the reader the sense that literature is sheer artifice. In part 2 of *Don Quixote of La Mancha,* the Errant Knight and Sancho are aware that part 1 of Cervantes' novel is in circulation not only in Spain but throughout Europe. Velázquez, in *Las meninas* (1656), paints himself into the picture, next to the Infanta Margarita and the meninas, Isabel Velasco and Agustina Sarmiento. And he includes a mirror in the background that makes clear that it's King Philip IV and Queen Mariana of Asturias who are looking at the scene. Theirs is the position of privilege. Through a mirrorlike reversal the viewer himself holds that position. The work has been written about endlessly. Among the best commentaries I know are by Foucault in his book *The Words and the Things*. Also, art critic Kenneth Clark, who wrote about Velázquez as well as Leonardo da Vinci and Piero della Francesca, said of *Las meninas* in his book *Looking at Pictures*, published in 1960,

Of course, we do not have to look for long before recognizing that the world of appearances has been politely put in its place. The canvas has been divided into quarters horizontally and sevenths vertically. The meninas and the dwarfs form a triangle of which the base is one-seventh of the way up, and the apex is four-sevenths; and within the large triangle are three subsidiary ones, of which the little Infanta is the centre. But these and other devices were commonplaces of workshop tradition. Any Italian hack of the seventeenth century could have done the same, and the result wouldn't have interested us. The extraordinary thing is that these calculations are subordinate to an absolute sense of truth. Nothing is emphasized, nothing forced. Instead of showing us with a whoop of joy how clever, how perceptive or how resourceful he is, Velázquez leaves us to make all these discoveries for ourselves. He does not beckon to the spectator any more than he flatters the sitter.

VA : The use of the mirror serves as a reference to a world ruled by appearances . . .

IS : Indeed, the mirror was a favorite artifact in Spain's Golden Age and is also ubiquitous in our time. Turn around and what are you likely to find but a mirror and yourself reflected in it? In Hispanic America, the mirror as symbol is a recurrent theme in the art of Frida Kahlo, Juan O'Gorman, and Remedios Varo (whose style is reminiscent of Jan van Eyck's *Portrait of Giovanni Arnolfini and His Wife* of 1434), and in the stories and poems of Jorge Luis Borges. It also makes a stellar appearance in Gabriel García Márquez's *One Hundred Years of Solitude.* The mirror is perceived not only as a vanity tool but as a door to another dimension, a bit like in Lewis Carroll's stories about Alice in Wonderland. Curiously, Jewish literature is far less interested in it.

VA : What is the cultural history of mirrors?

IS : The history of mirrors—which are nothing but sheets of glass coated on their back with aluminum or silver—is illustrative of how humans approach vanity. They were already present in antiquity (China, Egypt, Greece, Rome), although in a rudimentary form—as disks made of bronze, tin, or silver, for private use or decoration. They reflected the world in a rather evasive fashion. The Celts used them in the Middle Ages. In sixteenth-century Venice a technique was developed employing mercury. The metallic silver coating we're familiar with dates from 1835. It was the French who disseminated their use and turned their framing into works of art.

V A : What is the mirror's role in children's literature?

I S : Mirrors also appear in eighteenth-century folktales, such as
Snow White by the Brothers Grimm, which includes the famous line: "Mirror, mirror, on the wall . . ." In mythology and
children's tales the mirror represents a mysterious, somewhat
dangerous object, offering a lesson on false pride—as in the
myth of Narcissus. Or else, the mirror is a window to another
world. In Lewis Carroll's *Through the Looking Glass,* mirrors
are far from being objects of vanity and far from being always
benign.

V A : How does self-hatred relate to self-love?

I S : Just as Eros and Thanatos go together, self-love and self-hatred
function as inseparable opposites. Who doesn't dislike an aspect of oneself? Absolute beauty and absolute perfection are
unattainable. But in order for an individual to function, self-love
must prevail. Otherwise there's a break, resulting in asocial,
abnormal, even criminal behavior. Arguably the deepest, most
durable example of this tension is Shakespeare's Hamlet. What
other character in literature allows for such contradictions?
He's the ultimate actor, performing at all times, for himself and
for others. There's something of him in each of us. Not accidentally, Coleridge once said, "I have a smack of Hamlet myself, if I may say so." In general, love is a performance. And
self-love is the performance we enact primarily for our own
enjoyment.

v a : In Greek mythology, Erato, with her lyre or her crown of
       roses, is the muse of love poetry.

i s : The nineteenth-century American poet James G. Percival, in
       "An Ode to Music," described her as Cupid's muse. Ralph
       Waldo Emerson, in his *Dial Essays* of 1843, said, "Mr. Percival is
       an upright, soldierly, free-spoken man, very much of a patriot,
       hates cant, and does his best." Surely not a very flattering re-
       mark. In the mid-1800s, there were three brand names in Ameri-
       can poetry circles: William Cullen Bryant, Richard Henry
       Dana, and Percival. Were they listed alphabetically, or was Perci-
       val really the lesser of the three, as Emerson often claimed? The
       fact that he's almost totally forgotten today is, I guess, the best
       answer. In any case, his tribute to Erato is curious:

But when Erato brushed her flowery lute,
What strains of sweetness whispered in the wind!

Soft as at evening when the shepherd's flute
To tones of melting love alone resigned,
Breathes through the windings of the silent vale;
Complaining accents tremble on the gale,
Or notes of ecstasy serenely roll.
So when the smiling muse of Cupid sung,
Her melody sighed out the sorrowing soul,
Or o'er her silken chords
Sweet notes of gladness rung.

Does ecstasy roll serenely? Seldom, I think. Erato is the muse of lust and desire. When she's present, ecstasy rolls in like thunder. Ironically, she's also the muse of mimicry. In Hellenistic times, it was already clear that lovers are actors. The world is an empty stage, and the spotlight is on them. The play might start with a simple kiss and evolve into a ritualistic act of fusion. There are various mythological explanations for it. Strictly speaking, Eros is the Greek god of love, representing the force to live, to endure, to survive and multiply. In Aristophanes' play *The Birds,* Eros emerges out of an egg laid by Nyx (that is, Night). In the version by Hesiod called *Theogony,* Eros results from an encounter between the earth, the underworld, and Chaos. And subsequent interpretations present Eros as the son of Aphrodite. That the character is male is significant, designed to create trouble. He's paired with Psyche just as often as he's paired with Thanatos.

VA : You have yet to define the word *desire.*

I S : *Desire,* states the *OED,* is "the feeling or emotion which is directed to the attainment or possession of some object from which pleasure or satisfaction is expected." French intellectuals like Georges Bataille, who inherited from the nineteenth-century Romantics their appreciation of angst, used it incessantly. The pursuit of pleasure starts with the baby yearning for the mother's milk and mutates as the need for satisfaction becomes more sophisticated.

V A : What about the term *eroticism?*

I S : It was made fashionable by the French in the eighteenth century. It somehow turns the cult of Eros into a bourgeois doctrine, just as machismo, the sense of masculinity that includes excessive displays of confidence, virility, and even aggressiveness, became a Mediterranean attitude that spread throughout the Hispanic world. It's important to distinguish between love, eroticism, and sex. Although at times they appear indistinguishable—they all relate to our origin—they are essentially different forms of behavior. Love is the Platonic desire for union with another being. Eroticism is the discovery of another being's body and, following from that, the discovery of the pleasures of one's own body. Sex is copulation, designed as a form of survival. Humans find pleasure in sex and often make that pleasure the ultimate objective. But at its core, intercourse is about reproduction. Western religions are quite adamant about it. They make sure the sexual encounter isn't casual but sacred. If sex places humans in the animal kingdom, eroticism separates us from all other living creatures. No other mates explore the lover's body with such care and attention. No other mates experiment with sexual positions. No other mates concoct to achieve a greater degree of satisfaction.

V A : What's the difference between love and lust?

I S : In Old English, *lust* was a synonym for passionate desire. Today it represents the relentless appetite for sexual pleasure. The *OED* defines it thus: "Desire, appetite, relish or inclination for something." In modern times, it has become a synonym for uncontrollable sexual need. It's connected with the term *cupidity:* "Ardent desire, inordinate longing or lust." In Roman mythology, Eros is Cupid, the God of Love (and son of Mercury and Venus), a child deity usually depicted with a bow and arrow, representing the hunting of the lover's heart. In Hesiod's *Theogony,* Cupid was the result of the encounter between Chaos and the earth, although in another genealogy Cupid is the son of Zeus and Venus.

V A : Why is it that the classical Eros, the cupid with his quiver full of arrows, is a puerile image?

I S : It wasn't in the Middle Ages or the Renaissance. To a large extent, modernity has trafficked with love to exhaustion, making it look adolescent. Indeed, as Diane Ackerman points out in her book *A Natural History of Love,* people are somewhat embarrassed by love today and reluctant to admit to it, treating it as if it were obscene. The word itself often makes us stumble and blush. Ackerman believes that while as a society we have many a sharp verb to describe the gradations of hatred, the monosyllabic word *love* has neither gradations nor synonyms.

Cupid is the equivalent of the Greek myth of Eros. Cupid isn't an archetype of excess. He's love-struck, yes, and therefore incapable of mastering other emotions. Yet he isn't unjustified in his behavior. On Valentine's Day, the imagery of a childish Cupid is rather innocent.

VA : Talking about representations, Greek and Roman art is filled with nude images.

IS : In the pre-Christian age, nudity wasn't shameful. That shame is based on the biblical tale of Adam and Eve. Adam is the sole human inhabitant on the Almighty's creation, until God recognizes that he needs a companion. God makes Eve from one of Adam's ribs, and she becomes "bone of my bones, and flesh of my flesh." It is only after Eve, tempted by the serpent, eats from the forbidden Tree of Knowledge of Good and Evil, and gives Adam a taste as well, that they become aware of their nudity and feel shame. They then sew together fig leaves to make themselves loincloths. Given the often brutal heat in the Middle East, the prohibition against nudity isn't based on climate but on religious convention. Nudes are present in Egypt, Peru, and India, although not in all cultures. Martial makes fun of the prohibition in his cynical epigrams from the first century CE. Interestingly, while bareness, fertility, and genitalia are common in ancient art, depictions of human sexual behavior are rare. Think of the novel *The Golden Lotus*, written in 1618 by Xiaoxiaosheng, about a wealthy man who has four wives and sets out to acquire two more. It's based on an augmented version of a minor story in the medieval Robin

Hood-themed work entitled *Water Margin,* also known as *Outlaws of the Marsh,* written by Shi Nai-an and Luo Guanzhong sometime in the fourteenth century. *The Golden Lotus* is still banned in mainland China, and in the West prudishness has played its hand as well. When Clement Egerton first published his translation, in 1939, he rendered all the sexual passages in Latin, either by his own volition or under pressure from his publishers. But perhaps more interesting is *The Carnal Prayer Mat,* written by Li Yu in 1657 and translated in 1996 by Patrick Hanan. It's a masterful erotic satire in the guise of a series of moralistic tales about a scholar who wants to become a monk. In one story, for example, the scholar, in an attempt to seduce the local beauty, who is married to a man known to be well endowed, undergoes plastic surgery and has his penis replaced by that of a dog. What makes this collection of stories enormously pleasurable to read is that each story ends with a commentary, written ostensibly by a reviewer but most likely penned by none other than Li Yu, which infuses the oeuvre with wit and humor. In these and other examples, the descriptions of sexual activity are a revelation.

VA : How do you explain such chastity?

IS : I doubt that it's because sexual love has been deemed less important than other activities, such as cooking. Rather, I believe the answer is connected to taboos. Erotic art is the result of a slow, patient weakening of moral restrictions. In Western civilization, prohibition against obscenity was solid up until the Victorian age. In other cultures (though not in all), there was danger in the artistic portrayal of *amor veneris.* Sexual intercourse was private, intimate, and connected with origins. The excess of pleasure was linked to loss of control.

VA : Erotic art, in your view, is an exception then, not a rule.

IS : Yes. Eros is about origins. Where do we come from? How were we born? Even the most erotic of paintings, such as Gustav Klimt's *Danaë,* painted in 1907, are recondite. Klimt lived in Vienna at a time of intense sexual exploration. Indeed, some have described this period as one of surrendering moral standards. Klimt was a painter and illustrator closely associated with the art nouveau school. He did interior design, furniture, murals, and book covers. His art is about love and sex. *Danaë* has an extraordinary geometrical structure. Danaë's left thigh takes about a fourth of the canvas and is closest to the viewer physically. The torso is a vertical element tempting us with a view of her pudenda, which are only suggested. Her left hand is hidden, emphasizing the strong erotic nature of the piece by hinting at the location of the hand. It isn't accidental that Klimt's Danaë is red-haired. In medieval times red-haired women were symbols of Satan, promoters of lust and spreaders of evil. Her mouth is slightly open and her lower teeth visible, a sign of pleasure. The fingers of her right hand are open, resembling a spider about to crawl over the left breast, its nipple erect in anticipation. A seminal flow streams across Danaë's legs. This is a reference to the myth of Zeus mating with Danaë through showers of gold to produce a son, Perseus. And then there's the whimsical black rectangle, an out-of-context object, a vertical element to the left of Danaë's crotch. It could be seen as a mistake, but it isn't. Klimt has inserted an abstract reference to emphasize the realism of the painting. Is it a small penis, always tempting yet incapable in its size to satisfy her desire?

Equally interesting is the fact that Danaë seems to be, like Millais's Ophelia, underwater. Her hair looks as if it's floating. Is she in a bathtub? And what is represented by the two scarves, one to her right and one covering her left foot? It's an image of one awaiting submission. The purest part of her body is her left breast, the nipple forming the painting's center.

Another highly erotic artist is the Austrian expressionist Egon Schiele. (Mario Vargas Llosa, in his semipornographic novel *In Praise of the Stepmother*—he might want to call it erotic, but I have reservations—used Schiele as leitmotif for the husband and stepchild's quest to possess the female protagonist.) Schiele's life was filled with dramatic twists. His father suffered from dementia and died of syphilis when the painter was young. Schiele, an exhibitionist and a narcissist, had what appears to be an incestuous relationship with his younger sister, and he was a protégé of Klimt. He fought in the Great War and fell in love with two girls, marrying one and proposing to the other that they have a yearly escapade together. He and his wife, Edith, died of Spanish influenza within three days of each other. (I particularly like the painting *Death and the Maiden,* painted only a couple of years before his death in 1918.)

Schiele's painting *Fille aux jambes étendues* (1910) is emphatically erotic. He often made self-portraits, appearing nude. It's known that he sold regularly to collectors of pornographic art in Vienna. In particular, he was attracted to pubescent girls, who appear in works like *Semi-Nude Girl, Reclining* (1911). In a painting of himself and his wife, his pubic area is visible, though hers is not.

VA: You talked of an act of fusion evolving from a simple kiss . . .

IS: The kissing between a male and a female became an accepted expression of romantic love only rather recently in Western civilization. Physical contact wasn't encouraged in ancient times. In fact, in Judaism the Talmudic tractate Baba Metzia encourages the sexes to keep a distance. It also stresses the vulnerability of women as a factor that might cause trouble between couples. And it portrays the female sex as endowed with a wisdom that isn't intellectual but instinctive, even suggesting a natural connection between women and the divine. The tractate cautions, "Be careful not to make a woman weep, for God counts her tears." A spontaneous kiss between a man and a woman is forbidden.

Other cultures kiss for different reasons. The *OED* defines the word *kiss* thus: "To press or touch with the lips (at the same time compressing and then separating them), in token of affection, or greeting, or as an act of reverence." (I like the parenthetical information, as it resembles a kiss.) In other words, it's a form of salutation or caressing. In Old English it was *cuss,* and the verb was *cyssan;* the present tense, *cyste,* the past tense, *cyssed.* In Dutch it's *kussen;* in German *küssen.* For those not immersed in Western ways, the act of kissing might look strange. The facial gesture is rather comical: the tension of the lips to make a rounded protuberance, the noise emerging from the smashing of the internal part of the mouth, allowing an opening. The kiss isn't found in Asian, African, or Polynesian cultures, for instance. Judging from the Song of Songs, it must have been a fixture in Phoenician, Babylonian, and Canaanite societies, at least in the private realm. And the *Kama Sutra* also alerts us to its presence in India. In Shakespeare's *Antony and Cleopatra,* Antony evaluates the worth of one of Cleopatra's embraces:

Kingdoms are clay; our dungy earth alike
Feeds beast as man, the nobleness of life
Is to do thus; when such a mutual pair
And such a twain can do't, in which I bind. (1.1.35 – 38)

And in *Coriolanus,* the protagonist states: "O, a kiss / Long as my exile, sweet as my revenge!" (5.3.44 – 45). Among the best poems I know about kissing is Thomas Hardy's "Two Lips," from *Human Shows, Far Phantasies, Songs and Trifles:*

I kissed them in fancy as I came
    Away in the morning glow:
I kissed them through the glass of her picture-frame:
    She did not know.

I kissed them in love, in troth, in laughter,
  When she knew all; long so!
That I should kiss them in a shroud thereafter
  She did not know.

V A : One day somebody should write a cultural history of the kiss.

I S : It has been done. In the seventeenth century, the German
thinker Martin von Kempen compiled an encyclopedia of kissing, which he titled *Opus Polyhistoricum . . . de Osculis*. He
offered a nomenclature of some two dozen different types of
kisses, including a lover's kiss, the kissing of a religious icon,
a greeting kiss, the wedding ceremony kiss, the conciliatory
kiss, the mentoring kiss, the unmeant kiss, and, yes, *el beso de
Judas,* the traitor's kiss, named for Judah's last kiss to Jesus
Christ after selling him to the Romans for thirty pieces of silver
(according to the canonical gospels). It's possible, however, to
reduce Kempen's nomenclature to two: the ceremonial kiss
and the erotic kiss. The first is done in public for a variety of
reasons ranging from politics—the kissing of leaders during a
truce—to greetings. This type of kiss might be lip to lip but
more often takes place on the cheek or forehead, and as part of
an embrace. Think of the iconic black-and-white photo of the
returning sailor kissing the nurse, taken by Alfred Eisenstaedt
on V-J Day, 1945, in Times Square and featured in *Life* magazine. Nothing else matters to the couple: not the parade of
which they are part, not the weather . . . In this case, the kiss

isn't necessarily a preamble to sexual love; instead, it's an expression of joy. Victory over Japan has been accomplished!

The erotic kiss, by contrast, involves adrenaline. It's done to generate a degree of pleasure in the recipient and is an integral part of the sexual encounter. It could be lip to lip, as the *OED* says, but this definition is somewhat prudish. A better definition might be the pressing or touching of the lips as a stimulator.

But if the kiss is a beginning, it might also be a conclusion. In the frightful photograph made in 1990 by Joel-Peter Witkin called "The Kiss," the same face of an old man is reproduced twice—or are these two different individuals? Or is it one head severed in two during an autopsy and rearranged? Witkin is an American photographer, a New Yorker whose father was Jewish and his mother Roman Catholic. He has a twin brother (Jerome Witkin, also a significant figure in art). I read that Witkin credits his beginnings as a photographer to a terrifying scene: when he was a child, he witnessed an automobile accident that took place in front of his house in which a little girl was decapitated. "The Kiss" is a necrophilic scene, and the rest of Witkin's grotesque art is similarly haunting. It's invaded by hermaphrodites, monsters, and dreamlike sequences. It's in conversation with Hieronymus Bosch, Francisco de Goya, and surrealism. Witkin has a photograph of a woman with three nipples, images of disembodied and flagellated people, as well as a reinterpretation of Velázquez's *Las meninas.* In a 1996 piece in *World Art,* Witkin argued, "I think that what makes a photograph so powerful is the fact that, as opposed to other forms, like video or motion pictures, it's about stillness. I think the reason a person becomes a photographer is because they want to take it all and compress it into one particular stillness. When you really want to say something to someone, you grab them, you hold them, you embrace them. That's what happens in this still form." He also invoked Seamus Heaney, who, according to Witkin, said, "The end of art is peace." Witkin added, "It's a wonderful statement. The reason we go to museums and the reason we look at beautiful things is that there's not much out there that's beautiful any more. I think of museums as new kinds of religious centers, as spiritual centers of the secular life." Maybe by stating that there's nothing beautiful left, he establishes a connection between kissing and death.

VA: What about sucking? Is it another form of kissing?

IS: Maybe. To suck, states the *OED,* is "to draw (liquid, esp. milk from the breast) into the mouth by contracting the muscles of the lips, cheeks, and tongue, so as to produce a partial vacuum." The action of kissing is part of it, but the result is different. Kissing is about conveying affection, whereas sucking is about being nurtured. The primal act of sucking is part of breastfeeding. Doctors will tell you that sucking is a natural behavior, although some individuals need a little push in order to engage in it. Hippocrates believed that young animals forget in the course of a few days the art of sucking and cannot acquire it again without some difficulty. But the connection between the two, kissing and sucking, is more complex: the contact generated in the sucking of the breast remains ingrained in a person's being forever. Every sexual encounter includes, albeit marginally, a return to the primal act of being pleased through sucking from the mother's breast.

Both kissing and sucking involve bodily juices. These juices—sweat, saliva, semen—are an integral component of the sexual encounter. Letting them out of one's body and onto a lover's allows for various degrees of pleasure. The sucking of the sexual organs is an ancestral ritual. Again, different cultures practice it in their own way. It's known that in modern Papua New Guinea, eight-year-old boys are sent to all-male households to be fed "male food." The food in question is sperm, which they receive by performing fellatio on older men. It's done, apparently, to counteract the effects of all those years of eating food prepared by women. The tribe considers it another form of breastfeeding. According to Robert Stiller, a field psychoanalyst, the practice is carefully controlled. If an older boy attempted it on a younger boy, it wouldn't be sanctioned.

VA: Years ago I worked for a translation company. The owner called me to say that my last assignment had lost him a huge account, an HMO in California, because I had translated "breast cancer" into Spanish as the high register *cáncer de mama*. According to the HMO, I had used the word for fellatio. I learned my lesson: for the American market, I only use *cáncer de seno* now.

IS: The verb *to suck* has acquired a different meaning in the English language as of late. It seems that for American kids today, either things are great or they suck. Sucking up means paying homage to the big folks, whereas sucking down is paying attention to the little people.

VA : The myth of Eros, as you mentioned, evolves on Mount Olympus. What about eroticism in the Bible?

IS : The Old Testament is the ultimate source for appreciating love. What kind of love is on display? There's the love of the divine for his creatures, especially his chosen people, and its reciprocation. Indeed, the narrative might be described as a tumultuous romance between God and Israel.

The narrative in Genesis, chapters 1–3, is about shame and exile. Is it a love story? Not in the traditional sense. It isn't about two lovers but about four characters and a prop. The characters are Adam and Eve, God and the snake; the prop is the apple. The Almighty creates man "in his own image," then Eve from Adam's rib. Adam describes her as "bone of my bones, and flesh of my flesh." Genesis 2:24 states, "Therefore shall a man leave his father and his mother, and shall cleave unto his wife: and they shall be one flesh." The relationship between man and woman is portrayed as essential. At that point both are naked and "not ashamed." Next comes the tree, the serpent, and the apple, and discord enters the stage. Discord leads to shame, and shame to exile.

VA : Is discord the trigger?

IS : The plotline is shaped around a misunderstanding. Or else, a deliberate act of transgression. The Almighty establishes an elemental rule: don't eat from the tree. But prohibitions become temptations. The moment we're told not to engage in a particular form of behavior, an urge to do it takes over. It's an experience anyone with small children can relate to: the *don't* becomes the *why not*. Choice enters the picture. Ultimately, the story of Genesis is about choice. Why does Eve eat the apple? Is it because she falls prey to temptation? Yes, but temptation is a matter of choice. The narrative depicts her as impulsive. She doesn't ponder the consequences of her actions. Her choice, then, isn't made in an informed fashion. She succumbs to her instincts.

VA: Is the biblical story about evil?

IS: I would ask the question in another way. Is evil an external force, lurking in the world in order to make us fall? That's the approach that prevailed until the Enlightenment. Humans were neutral. It was the environment that pushed them in the direction of good or of evil. The modern conception is different. The struggle between opposite forces takes place inside us. The assumption is that knowledge will ultimately lead you to the control of passion—reason and passion, Psyche and Eros.

VA: Eve isn't evil. She's simply unaware of her limits.

IS: She's unaware of self-control. Supposedly, Judaism, unlike Greek culture, isn't filled with mythological characters. That, however, is a superficial assessment. Take the character of Lilith. From the outset, her existence is problematic. She doesn't show up in Genesis, although Isaiah 34:14 does make reference to her. She was an Assyrian siren and is seen in Jewish lore as "the demon of the night" that snatches up children. In Greek mythology, the equivalent might be Lamia. In any case, Lilith is supposed to have been Adam's first wife, after she cohabited with Satan. She's also described as the mother of all demons. In Kabbalah, she's represented as promiscuous and hypersexual. Feminists have taken to Lilith because of her irreverence and independence of spirit.

VA : What other biblical episodes are there about passionate love?

IS : Most episodes are about partnering for reproductive purposes. They are defined, albeit torturously, by consent: Jacob and Leah and Rachel, Tobias and Sara, Amnon and Tamar, Judith and Holofernes, Joseph and Potiphar's wife, Ruth and Boaz, Abraham and Hagar, Moses and Zipporah, Ahab and Isabel, and more. The liaison between Samson and Delilah, however, is about passion and the excess of testosterone.

VA : Machismo?

IS : Perhaps. It's important to keep in mind, though, that from Adam and Eve on, sexual encounters in the Bible are described tangentially, as means of reproduction. The liaisons of the three patriarchs—Abraham, Isaac, and Jacob—and the four matriarchs—Sarah, Leah, Rachel, and Rivkah—are consistently about the duty to pair and multiply.

The Bible does make exceptions, most importantly in the Shir ha-Shirim, which, based in the King James Version, is known variously as the Song of Songs, the Song of Solomon, Canticles, and even the Canticle of Canticles. It contains some of the most beautiful verses in the Bible, but they are puzzling.

Early Jewish and Christian scholars attempted to explain them by agreeing that these verses couldn't possibly depict worldly love. But are they about eroticism?

To answer, I need first to talk about the process of canonization of the Bible. There were books left out of the Old and New Testaments. Among those that were included, many take an alternative narrative pattern; the Book of Job, for instance. The vast majority of biblical tales aren't about a single character, even a patriarch like Abraham, Isaac, or Jacob, but about a character's genealogy. The tale of Job takes an unusually modern approach. It's Kafkaesque avant la lettre in that it chronicles the inner life of an average person victimized by the Almighty. The character of Satan makes a small but fateful appearance, which is an anachronism in a text pushing its monotheistic message. But anachronisms abound in the Bible. The Song of Songs is a suitable example. It has been portrayed as an allegory of the love of the Almighty for the people of Israel. But allegory is no longer an attractive way to solve the enigma. Contemporary critics believe that the references to King Solomon were an afterthought, added to explain, even to rationalize, his role. It appears, based on the style and cadence, that the poems were written half a century after Solomon's reign, quite possibly by numerous hands and with a unifying motif. In short, the Song of Songs appears to be an anthology of erotic poetry manipulated so as to make it into the canon.

VA: Solomon, it is said, had seven hundred wives and three hundred concubines.

I S : His sexual life, then, fits well in the context. But metaphor only takes us that far. To modern readers the literal meaning of the biblical narrative is unavoidable. It's true that the verses are an example of indirect, poetic language. But they are about earthly encounters, no doubt. Consider the following lines from cantos 1:2–3:

Let him kiss me with the kisses of his mouth:
for thy love is better than wine.

Because of the savour of thy good ointments
thy name is as ointment poured forth,
therefore do the virgins love thee.

Or these lines, from canto 4:16:

Awake, O north wind;
and come, thou south;
blow upon my garden,
that the spices thereof may flow out.
Let my beloved come into his garden,
and eat his pleasant fruits.

The King James translators insert titles into the chapters, making arbitrary references to a bride, a bridegroom, a marriage, a separation and reunion. But the material isn't about marriage; it's about erotic encounters, their ups and downs. The imagery couldn't be more visual, as in cantos 5:4–6:

My beloved put in his hand by the hole of the door, and my bowels were moved for him.

I rose up to open to my beloved; and my hands dropped with myrrh, and my fingers with sweet smelling myrrh, upon the handles of the lock.

I opened to my beloved; but my beloved had withdrawn himself, and was gone: my soul failed when he spake: I sought him, but I could not find him; I called him, but he gave me no answer.

Cantos 8:6–7 offer the leitmotif of love being stronger than death:

Set me as a seal upon thine heart, as a seal upon thine arm: for love is strong as death; jealousy is cruel as the grave: the coals thereof are coals of fire, which hath a most vehement flame.

Many waters cannot quench love,
neither can the floods drown it:
if a man would give all the substance of his house for love,
it would utterly be contemned.

In using subterfuges, the poem delves into scenes of passion
and torment. Jealousy plays a role in the encounter of the
lovers, who are at times described as brother and sister. The
act of finding and missing each other gives the narrative its
pathos.

The Song of Songs is typical of the genre called epithalamia, written in ancient times by Pindar, Catullus, and Sappho,
who was called by Plato "the tenth muse." In 1595, one sees it
again in Edmund Spenser's "Epithalamium," written to celebrate his own marriage. An epithalamion is a ritual song, and it
has an element of sacred magic about it; it becomes itself a
kind of wedding rite. The name is derived from the Greek
words *epi* (on, upon) and *thalamos* (room, bridal chamber),
and the ancient examples of the genre were designed to be
sung in the threshold of the bridal chamber. In terms of form
they often use a refrain or repetition. In terms of theme they
are full of classical allusions, especially to Juno, the goddess of
childbearing, and Hymen, the god of marriage. Of the many
conventions available to these poets, some of the most commonly used are the consummation of the marriage as a harvest,
the defloration of the bride as strife, and the warding off of
malevolent forces. Then there's John Donne's "Epithalamion

Made at Lincoln's Inn." Canonical forms are designed to be revamped, to be messed around with. Cervantes revamped the *novela caballeresca,* and Donne the epithalamia. Lincoln's Inn was a law school where Donne was enrolled for several years. The students, all male, had raucous celebrations where they played the roles of the bride and groom, so many scholars think that the "Epithalamion Made at Lincoln's Inn" is a parody of the genre.

VA : Do you recall when you first read the Song of Songs?

IS : I don't. It was probably in Hebrew, although I remember it best in Spanish.

VA : Didn't Fray Luis de León translate it?

IS : Yes. In the sixteenth century, Fray Luis de León, an Augustine monk and the son of conversos, devoted part of his career to a Spanish translation of the Song of Songs. And he was imprisoned for it. In March 1572 the Holy Office of the Inquisition had him arrested and sent to the dungeons in Valladolid. There were many reasons why Fray Luis may have been closely watched, including his Jewish ancestry. He must have been put under especially heavy surveillance when it became known not only that he had Jewish blood but that he preferred the Hebrew Bible over the Vulgate. Imprisonment was swift, not because he had translated the Song of Songs per se, but because the Council of Trent forbade the translation of sacred texts—any sacred texts—into vulgar tongues. Like Joseph K., the protagonist of Kafka's *The Trial,* Fray Luis was kept in a cell for five years without being notified of the charges. He wrote his best poems there, such as this one about God's love (translated into English by Thomas Walsh):

Aquí la envidia y la mentira
me tuvieron encerrado.
Dichoso el humilde estado
del sabio que se retira
de aqueste mundo malvado,
y con pobre mesa y casa
en el campo deleitoso
con sólo Dios se compasa,
y a solas su vida pasa,
ni envidiado ni envidioso.

[Lo, where envy and where lies
Held me in the prison cell:
Blessed was the lot that fell
To the humble and the wise
Far from earth's chagrins to dwell;
Who with thatch and homely fare
Rests him in some sylvan spot,
Lone with God abiding there,
And none else his thought to share,
Envying none, and envied not.]

VA: What about eroticism in the Kabbalah?
IS: The mystical tradition in Judaism is replete with erotic im-

agery. Not accidentally was it proscribed from the mainstream. Kabbalists are often portrayed as obsessive types, focusing on the connection between the human body and the universe. The power and structure of the ten Sephiroth, with their neo-Platonic function of emanating energy, are supposedly designed to produce orgasmic joy when in perfect equilibrium. And the encounter between the male part of the divine and its female counterpart, known as the Shekhinah, also has a sexual component. In the Zohar, written apocryphally in Spain by Moisés de León (it was actually credited to Rabbi Jonathan ben Zachai), the suggestion is made that these two parts shall remain separate as long as their offspring, the people of Israel, remain in exile. The Shekhinah accompanies its children until their return to the Promised Land takes place once and for all. In short, the cosmos for Jewish mystics is a playing field of erotic forces. There are plenty of variations to this interpretation, including antinomianism.

v a : What is antinomianism?

i s : It's a philosophy that encourages sin as a form of sanctification. One of the most famous antinomians connected—albeit loosely—with Jewish mysticism is Jacob Frank, a Jewish merchant also known as the Baron of Offenbach, who died in 1791. He believed himself to be the messiah and was connected with the pseudo-messiah Shabbetai Zevi, a leader who in 1666 promised that the cosmos would be redeemed by God but then converted to Islam around the time of the prophesied moment. Gershom Scholem wrote a biography of him. Some of Shabbetai Zevi's followers, convinced that their leader had only superficially transgressed, began an antinomian religion based on lewd behavior, including rape and various types of crime.

VA : Let's leave transgression for later.

IS : No problem—it's a timeless topic.

VA : In *On Borrowed Words,* you recall your sexual initiation. But the scene doesn't seem to be about love. Do you remember the moment you discovered love's "extremes," as you've called them: attraction and repulsion, exultation and misery?

IS : For me love and literature have always been interconnected. Years ago, while still in Mexico, I read Denis de Rougemont's book *L'Amour et l'Occident* in French. It was about how Petrarca, even more than Plato, defined the way Western civilization approaches love. De Rougemont's style is self-important, grandiose. In any case, I remember reading it just after I had finished Mario Vargas Llosa's comic novel *Aunt Julia and the Scriptwriter,* which is about a semi-incestuous relationship between Marito, the author's alter ego, and his aunt. At one point Marito says something about Petrarca, something to the effect that he *invented* our views on love.

VA : That's the exact word you use in *Dictionary Days.*

IS : The Talmudic tractate Sanhedrin states that "love destroys one's mental equilibrium." It also argues that "for a little love you can pay with your life." I almost did. I remember being puzzled. Love isn't a scientific invention, like penicillin or electricity. I needed some context. So I read Petrarca's *Canzoniere* and, soon after, de Rougemont's rumination. It was a rather impressionable period in my life. I was eager to understand—to describe rationally—what I was experiencing. You see, around that time I had fallen madly for an older Parisian woman—let me call her Brigitte—who had come to Mexico to study. I had been in love before with *una niña bien,* but that was an inconsequential relationship, in retrospect. It was a conventional liaison, a friendship, really. My relationship with Brigitte was the opposite. It isn't that I was not in control of myself; the image presupposes the possibility of chaos, that is, the overriding of all rational thinking. I was under the sign of passion—passion running amok, on the verge of insanity. None of that was possible with *la niña bien.* Every time I was with Brigitte, I was shaken by a sense of oceanic emotion, a feeling of being beyond myself, as if I had become part of the cosmos. *Fuego,* fire—no other images come quicker to mind . . . Someone gave me a copy of the *Kama Sutra,* and we used it in our physical explorations. Do I remember what her mind was like, how she processed thought? Brigitte was intelligent, but that part of her didn't interest me. It was her body I was hypnotized by: the lines of her profile, the shape of her hair, her minute breasts, the tactile sensation every time my hands touched her waist. I couldn't get enough of her. I sought words to survey my inner landscape. I even challenged myself to write poetry. But I'm no poet. Language for me is an instrument for surveying ideas, not for singing to what Shakespeare, in a superbly baroque twist, referred to as "love's labour's lost."

VA: How long did the relationship last?

IS: In chronological time, maybe a year. An eternity in existential time. But every night was its own circle of creation. I was ecstatic while those nights lasted. The moment they finished, I was fearful. Anna Akhmatova's poem about separation, "I Wrung My Hands," written in Kiev in 1911 and translated from the Russian by Stanley Kunitz, is perfect. The first quatrain is given here:

Сжала руки под темной вуалью . . .
«Отчего ты сегодня бледна?»
—Оттого, что я терпкой печалью
Напоила его допьяна.

[I wring my hands under my dark veil . . .
"Why are you pale, what makes you reckless?"
—Because I have made my loved one drunk
With an astringent sadness.]

While I lived through the encounters, I recall thinking to myself: I must remember all this in detail. One day I'll write about it, and my only source will be memory.

VA: Have you?

IS: Not yet.

VA: Will you?

IS: Maybe you've just gotten me started.

VA: Did the readings that occupied you then—Shakespeare, de

Rougemont, Petrarca, Vargas Llosa—change your encounters with Brigitte?

I S : They only intensified them. Literature isn't therapy; it's not meant to cure. It's only useful as a form of empathy, making you realize that however unique you might believe the threshold you're about to cross to be, others have gone through it before—and left inspired testimony of it.

V A : What happened in the end?

I S : The French have a memorable expression: *l'amour fou.* My descent into madness left a lasting impression. It took me a long time to recover. For years I would see Brigitte in dreams, the Brigitte of the past: svelte, sardonic, tempestuous . . . I wished I could have kept those images; they had become some sort of sustenance. But not long ago, on a trip to Biarritz, France, I saw her again. She looked different—heavier, more mature—and I did too. The encounter somewhat spoiled the memory. It's difficult to invoke the Brigitte of the past without superimposing the silhouette I came across in Biarritz. For some reason, she had acquired a copy of de Rougemont's book in English translation and had saved it for me. I was grateful but disillusioned. Brigitte was a French part of my Spanish past, but I had now switched to English as my primary language. I unconsciously felt an instinctive rejection of the English translation of the book. As I browsed through it I picked up on a number of liberties the translator had taken, beginning with the title: *Passion and Society.* I always thought

I had been in love with Brigitte, but perhaps I was simply consumed by passion.

VA : You mentioned the *Kama Sutra*. Erotic manuals are as ancient as the need to experience pleasure in copulation.

IS : They are part of the so-called science of sexuality, also known as erotology, an absurd term that seems to me closer to astrology than to anatomy. It's a word used by Sir Richard Burton, who translated the *Kama Sutra*, arguably the most famous of the ancient erotic manuals. Written by Mallanaga Vatsyayana sometime between the fourth and sixth centuries, the *Kama Sutra*—from *kama*, desire in Sanskrit, and *sutra*, thread—is a compendium of recommendations for sexual behavior. The word *science* is invoked throughout, suggesting that the different liaisons (with wives, courtesans, and others), and the various positions of intercourse, generate a hierarchy of pleasure. Yet I'm skeptical. There's nothing scientific in love; likewise, sexual intercourse might be reduced to a directory of positions, but its essence, the *fuego* that propels it, remains elusive. Since my affair with Brigitte I've reopened more than once the *Kama Sutra* in Burton's translation: it's flat and unpoetic—a bore, really. Its descriptions are about mechanics. One would expect a religious component, but there is none.

VA : Burton also translated *The Thousand and One Nights*.

IS : He was a fascinating nineteenth-century British adventurer, soldier, polyglot, diplomat, orientalist, linguist, poet, translator, and hypnotist, as well as a charlatan and a drunk. It is said that he spoke twenty-nine different European, Asian, and African languages. He traveled to Mecca and to central Africa. He once declared, "I'm proud to say I have committed every sin in the Decalogue." His translation of the *Kama Sutra* (1883) is the most interesting, if not necessarily the most successful, of a rather uninteresting text. The other ancient sexual manuals I'm acquainted with are the *Ananga Ranga,* composed by Kalyana Malla in 1172 and designed to prevent a split between spouses, and the sixteenth-century Arabic catalogue *The Perfumed Garden for the Soul's Recreation.* Burton translated both of these as well, in 1885 and 1887 respectively. He titled the latter *The Perfumed Garden of the Sheikh Nefzawi: A Manual of Arabian Erotology.*

V A : The *Kama Sutra* is often seen out of context.

I S : This is because there's little information about Vatsyayana, who apparently was a celibate scholar and maybe a philosopher, or about the Sanskrit culture that surrounded him.

V A : What was taking place in Western civilization then?

I S : Roughly, the *Kama Sutra* appeared as the Book of Revelations was inspiring St. John the Divine in his prison in Patmos. The *Ananga Ranga* came out more than five centuries ago, as Christopher Columbus was crossing the Atlantic Ocean.

V A : Is there an equivalent to the *Kama Sutra* in the Kabbalistic tradition?

I S : Not that I know of. The rabbinical tradition, on the other hand, includes sexually explicit, if also sarcastic, books such as *The Alphabet of Ben-Sira.*

VA: Earlier in our conversation you mentioned the archetypal pairing of Eros and Thanatos. Let's return to the topic . . .

IS: An attraction of opposites. In Apuleius's *Metamorphoses* we are also told the story of Eros and Psyche, as curious a coupling of hormones and neurons as there ever was. This type of pairing isn't uncommon: Isis and Osiris, Inanna and Dumuzi, Shiva and Sati, Layla and Majnun, and Tristan and Iseult. Eros and Thanatos have come to represent a balancing act between the forces of life and the forces of death. Love is, in general, part of the former. Thanatos—in Greek, Θάνατος, and to the Romans, Mors—is the personification of death. He—the mythological representation is male, sometimes depicted as a winged boy and other times as a swordsman—is the son of Nyx. To Freud *thanatos* is the death instinct.

Bataille wrote, "It surely seems that the presentiment of death determines our affective life." His preoccupation with the relationship between Eros and Thanatos led him to explore the ecstasy of the great sadists—Erzsébet Báthory, Doña Catalina de los Ríos y Lísperguer, Gilles de Rais—as well as the permanent taste of the crowd for the cruelest spectacles of death.

I don't know why but whenever I think of Thanatos, the art of lampoonist José Guadalupe Posada comes to mind. He was a darling of surrealists like André Breton, who in turn were inspired by Freud's concept of the death instinct. Posada is surely unique in his depiction of death.

VA: In your book *The Riddle of Cantinflas,* you include an essay on Posada.

I S : His most recurrent character is the *calavera catrina,* a joyful skeleton recalling medieval depictions of death with a sarcastic twist. Posada's calaveras are irreverent. They ridicule the bourgeoisie and the political establishment at the end of the nineteenth century and as the Mexican Revolution of 1910 unfolds. But they also laugh at the idleness of the masses, who are always broke and who drink too much. In the lithograph *Fiesta de calaveras* (1908), Posada offers a reversal of the traditional social scene. Is this what death will do to us? Or is he suggesting that we are, at every point, "presentes sucesiones de difunto," in Quevedo's words, loosely translated as present successions of death?

V A : How did Freud's successors present the death instinct?

I S : In large part, the continued connection between Eros and Thanatos in modern discussions on love has been a result of Freud's theories of the mind and of the impact his pupils and descendants have had, including Carl Gustav Jung, Otto Rank, Wilhelm Fliess, Alfred Adler, Melanie Klein, and even Freud's daughter, Anna Freud. The tension between the drive to live, to thrive, to excel, to love and be loved, to mate and redeem oneself, and the pull to be motionless, to acquiesce, to conclude, to die is Freud's line of thought.

When I was young and still in Mexico, one of Freud's disciples, Erich Fromm, who died in 1980, lived in Cuernavaca. His books were available in workmanlike translations released by the state-run publishing house, Fondo de Cultura Económica. I remember being impressed by his writings on childhood and adolescence, on the role toys play in human life, on rituals, and by his character studies of Martin Luther and Mahatma Gandhi. Knowing he was barely sixty miles away, I considered the possibility of visiting him in order to chat. One of the pieces— was it a full-length book?—that most affected me introduced two words I had not yet heard and, as it happens, have heard only once or twice altogether since then: *thanatophilia* and *thanatophobia,* although Fromm preferred to use the terms *necrophilia* and *necrophobia.*

V A : Did Fromm invent them?

I S : Maybe. Dread and trepidation toward death are an essential part of life, but necrophobia, as defined by the medical profession, is an excess of them. It's a phobia, with its necessary symptoms such as nausea, shaking, breathlessness, and loss of control. Conversely, necrophilia is an excessive love of death. As I remember it, there was something fluffy, unconvincing about Fromm's oeuvre; I've never felt the need to revisit it. I do recall that his approach to necrophilia was through an explanation of unstable personalities, such as Adolf Hitler, and serial killers, whose lives are justified by bringing about the death of others.

V A : The Hungarian writer Sándor Márai, who lived in San Diego, California, wrote in his book *Embers,* translated in 2001, that *to kill* and *to embrace* share an etymology in Hungarian.

I S : Yes, Márai made the connection between *öl* and *öllel.* Attila József, a poet, Hungarian too (he died in 1937), also pointed it out. And Károly Tar, a contemporary poet, wrote a poem called "Gyász," in English "Mourning," that plays on these words: *öllel öl,* to kill with the lap, or embrace. It's quite tempting to connect the two—another example of the natural link between Eros and Thanatos—but according to Hungarian linguists I've talked to, the words don't share an etymology. *Öl* as a verb is of Finno-Ugric origin and from the Ural era. The basis for this word was *wede,* which went through a lot of changes before it became today's *öl,* meaning "to kill, destroy, or spend an unusually large amount of money, time, and so on." The same root with the same meaning appeared in other languages of the same family. *Öl* as a noun is also of Finno-Ugric origin and could also be from the Ural era. The original form is thought to be *sile/süle,* and the original meaning of the word was supposed to be "two outstretched arms, the distance between the two, or even two circling arms." It also means "a bundle" (the amount you can hold in your arms). The word *ölelni,* to hug, comes from the latter. The suffix "l" forms verbs out of nouns, usually meaning some act performed with a part of the body.

VA : In your architectonic view of love, what's the locus of Eros in the house?

IS: The bedroom, the ultimate space for intimacy regardless of cultural differences. The home in general might be a symbol of privacy, but the bedroom has an exclusivity to it. In its modern conception, it contains a chest, a bed, a mirror, and a bathroom nearby. Its drapes are closed to emphasize privacy. It's where lovers find themselves alone, the theater where love and sexuality come together. And within the bedroom, the bed is sacrosanct.

I don't know if anyone has written a cultural history of the bedroom. Did the Egyptians conceive of it as we do? What about the Byzantine Empire? I suspect that, while the Carpathians, Babylonians, and Phoenicians already approached the bedroom as an individual space, the rise of Catholicism, with its prescriptive approach to monogamist love, consolidated its status in Western civilization.

va: The bedroom is also the domain of marriage.

is: In history, marriage becomes tied to love only with the advent of Christianity. In the Bible the connection between spouses has a concrete purpose: the perpetuation of the species and the protection of blood lines. The widow is forced to marry the brother of her deceased husband. Marriage also came about as a stable system to secure property rights and as a financial arrangement. In certain societies today, marriage might still be by proxy, and a dowry is involved. Or else, the buying of the bride takes place in a series of sophisticated gift exchanges. The concept of courtship is rather recent, and so is the idea that there ought to be love between a man and a woman. Indeed, it was Paul who transformed the partnership from a civil to a sacramental union, comparing a marriage to the relationship between Christ and his church and injecting the idea of love into it. And as the sacramental union was established, a domain of privacy between spouses came about.

As the cornerstone of Islam, the Qur'an rejects celibacy and emphasizes the importance of marriage. It uses the word *zawaj,* meaning a pair, to denote it. The Qur'an states, "And

Allah has made for you your mates of your own nature, and made for you, out of them, sons and daughters and grandchildren, and provided for you sustenance of the best" (16:72). It also says, "And among His signs is this, that He created for you mates from among yourselves, that you may dwell in tranquility with them, and He has put love and mercy between your hearts. Undoubtedly in these are signs for those who reflect" (30:21).

Western civilization's traditional understanding of marriage isn't only as a moral and legal institution but as a communion based on knowledge—physical, emotional, and intellectual. To have a spouse is to be in partnership, to form "a union." In Shakespeare's *The Merry Wives of Windsor,* Slender, when presented with the idea of marrying Anne Page, says, "If there be no great love in the beginning, yet heaven may decrease it upon better acquaintance, when we are married and have more occasion to know one another" (1.1.246–249). The *OED* defines marriage as a nuptial ceremony as well as "the condition to being a husband or a wife." The source is probably the twelfth-century French term *mariage,* although there's also a connection to the Spanish word (now out of use) *maridaje.* The word denoted the condition of spousehood, the liaison between husband and wife. The issue of consent plays a major role.

Yet the institution itself has never been static. Even though it remains the glue holding society together, the relationship between spouses has loosened up somewhat. The reason might be the relaxation of religious rules. In the Victorian era, a more critical view of marriage emerged based on a conviction that the union was defined by stilted social conventions. This was the moment when religion as a cohesive force in Western civilization began to crumble. But in fact, the Greeks and Romans recognized the institution of divorce—each in its own way approached it rather liberally, recommending that "matrimonia debent esse libera." It was, once again, the Christian Church that endorsed a strict prohibition against the spousal separation. If marriage was sacramental, only God could break it. From the tenth century onward, divorce wasn't allowed. It has taken almost a millennium for marriage to become a free-flowing liaison, although it is still defined by the protection of blood lines and by the system of property ownership. (By the way, I read somewhere that more than 25 percent of murders in the world happen between married couples.)

As Christianity consolidated its worldwide domain, Judaism and Islam followed along. In poetry, especially in *ghazals,* which began in Persia in the tenth century as a series of rhymed couplets accompanied by a refrain, the pleasant resignation that marriage requires becomes the topic. Interestingly, these Oriental lyrics structured in recurring lines are often about erotic life. But they might also address the durability of marriage or in general the torment of a relationship as in this example, by the sixteenth-century poet Ahmed-i Daʻî, from an anthology of Ottoman lyrical poetry translated by Walter G. Andrews, Najaat Black, and Mehmet Kalpaklı:

The torture of the beloved is no punishment
　　at all
Thank God for the faithfulness of your cruelty
There are many beloveds with cypress-bodies,
　　witch-eyes, and trouble-making brows
But not one of them has been so enticing
　　as you!

If those who thirst for the wine of your rubied lips
　　gave one thousand lives
One thousand lives for just the dregs—
　　it would be cheap!

No matter how much I am separated from you,
　　no matter how far
Your image remains constant within my soul

Oh my beloved, why do you withhold our union?
It does not befit you to torment your slave
　　this way!

Do a favor for the lovers, bring joy and captivate
　　their hearts
One must be faithful, for we know beauty
　　does not last

From my heart, I love you dearly,
　　more than life itself

Believe me, God knows there is no error

    in what I say

The temptation the lover's body generates in the poet
becomes a source of cruelty as well as a celebration of the
almighty. The poet portrays himself as a slave, a worshipper
of beauty, and a resister in the torture that is love.

An emblematic depiction of love and marriage inside the
bedroom is displayed in a painting I saw at the National Gallery
while I lived in London: Jan van Eyck's *Portrait of Giovanni
Arnolfini and His Wife.* It depicts the 1434 marriage of the Italian merchant Giovanni di Nicolao Arnolfini to Giovanna Ce-
nami, who was herself a merchant's daughter. That profession
affords the couple their high social status. The Flemish painter,
who met Arnolfini in Bruges, wouldn't have been doing this
kind of "wedding certificate" and serving as witness—the couple
married in a private room rather than in a religious setting—for
members of a less worthy class. In the background, a signature
reads in Latin, "Jan van Eyck was present." There's a frightening sternness in the couple's expression. Although they hold
hands, their connection isn't one of love but of convention. Is
there passion between them? If there is, the painter isn't interested in including it. Their eyes are half closed, as if announcing boredom. Is this what the future holds for the Arnolfinis?
Giovanni looks at us while Giovanna looks toward him, but her
attention seems somewhat lost. She's also pregnant. Is this the
reason Giovanna seems detached? Is it the reason for her marriage? The *Portrait* is a typical Flemish piece in its use of light

and color. The window is on the left, allowing the sun's rays to reflect on the skin of the subjects and to highlight the red, green, white, and brown of the fabric on the bed and their clothes. Giovanni's hat is huge, a symbol of his increasing status. Giovanna's head cover is a symbol of the sanctity of marriage. Aside from these symbols, there's a plethora of others: the dog represents loyalty, the shoes earthiness, and the chandelier hope.

The painting also includes a circular mirror, right above the couple's joined hands. An astonishing work of concentrated symbolism, the mirror is in a carved frame made of medallions, each including a miniature scene from the life of Christ. The mirror reflects the couple as seen from the back—an effect similar to Velázquez's—and, in front of them, van Eyck inserts a self-portrait. Unlike the artist in *Las meninas,* however, he has no canvas. And he's accompanied by someone else. Who is the person? It could be the priest officiating in the ceremony. Or might it be us, the viewers? Whatever the answer, it seems clear that the bedroom, as portrayed by van Eyck, isn't an erotic place. Instead, it's the stage where the social arrangement between spouses is consummated.

VA : The spouses as co-conspirators, then.

IS : Today, marriage is more connected with privacy than with sacramental union. Think of Grant Wood's controversial painting *American Gothic,* first exhibited at the Art Institute of Chicago in 1930. Is it about marriage? Maybe in the American style. It's a striking image of family relations that might be used as a Rorschach test. Are the subjects husband and wife? What kind of dry, puritanical relationship keeps them together? I've asked middle schoolers to reflect on the painting. The consensus is that it's a depiction of a New England couple. In fact, Wood was from Iowa, and the cottage in the background, in Gothic Revival style, was inspired by one he saw in a small Iowa town called Eldon. The upper part of the cottage is painted after a medieval pointed arch. The farmers, according to Grant, are meant to be a father and his unmarried daughter. Grant asked his own sister and his dentist to pose for him. Is the message about the repressed lives of families in small rural towns in America? Or is it instead about pride and the upholding of tradition? The power of *American Gothic* lies in the fact that it offers no easy answers. What is unquestionable is that the connection between father and daughter, as presented by Wood, isn't about warmth but about stoicism.

VA : Are marriage contracts proof that love is tangible?

IS : Such formalities don't allow love to be ruled by chance. They formalize, record, and catalog it. Ironically, wedding certificates (in Hebrew, *ketubot*) are the most unpoetic documents one is likely to find.

VA : Is marriage a domesticated form of love, then?

IS : It's about acquiescence. Eros and marriage are separate. Eros is approached by Western civilization as a source of passion. The permanent union between spouses is defined by genealogy and economics. Just before I got married, a friend of the family took me aside and said, "Ilan, can passion and patience coexist? If so, your marriage will be successful."

v a : When did you get married?

i s : In 1988. Alison and I met while working at the library of the Jewish Theological Seminary, in New York City, where we were both students. Ours was a secret love. She was employed as staff; I was a graduate student shelving books. We would open the library together and spend time chatting before proceeding to our respective duties. From the start the relationship was romantic. It has remained so ever since, through the births of our children and endless other occasions. You asked if marriage is a form of domesticated love. It is, but not in a derogatory way. Humans aren't made to be in a state of constant arousal. And whatever definition of passion one endorses includes the concept of time. Passion is consumed by the moment! But lasting relationships are hard to come by—especially in an age such as ours that is allergic to anything that lasts longer than a day. I'm madly in love with Alison. She's far more intuitive than I am, more sensitive to the environment. I've found intellectual and emotional stability with her. I couldn't conceive of myself pursuing diverse endeavors without such an anchor. You accompany one another. We've become partners in the seasons of life. I rejoice at the idea of having her at my side as I grow older. And I thrive on witnessing how she, too, distills her talents with age. We're at once companions and colleagues, never running out of topics to debate.

v a : It sounds like you've found lasting love.

i s : And a love that is comforting, too.

III

v a : You've said that dictionaries are prudish and unromantic.

i s : The definitions one encounters in them are as cold as ice. I often wonder: Do lexicographers ever feel the need to express themselves in a more poetic language? Do they get the blues?

v a : They are methodical.

i s : They are cold fish, and wimps, too.

v a : In *Dictionary Days,* you mention the reluctance of lexicography to indulge in offensive language. Might one not say the same about sexuality?

i s : Yes. Lexicographers are aware of their moral standing. They are fearful of censorship. But there are a few exceptions. Samuel Johnson included a raunchy poem by Jonathan Swift to define *fart* in his *A Dictionary of the English Language,* but he did not specifically include cant or sexual terminology. Ambrose Bierce's *The Devil's Dictionary* is risqué, to say the least, but it isn't so much a lexicon as a parody of lexicons, a word list.

VA: Do you consider there to be any true lexicons of sexuality?

IS: There are a number of them, but they differ from the *OED* or the *Diccionario de la lengua* in that they lack official endorsement. They have been compiled by rogues and mavericks. I find Mark Morton's *The Lover's Tongue* juicy, and Hernán Rodríguez Castelo's *Lexicón sexual ecuatoriano y latinoamericano* flat but informative. I've seen a facsimile of *The Dictionary of the Vulgar Tongue: A Dictionary of Buckish Slang, University Wit and Pick Pocket Eloquence,* published in 1811 by, of all possible organizations, an entity called the Canting Academy. There's also Rod L. Evans's *Sexicon* of 2002, which includes the wonderful *goy toy,* a slang term for an uncircumcised penis. Among the most inspiring of the bunch, in my eyes, is Camilo José Cela's three-volume *Diccionario secreto,* a thesaurus of forbidden words and expressions published in 1968. Cela, author of *The Family of Pascual Duarte* and *The Hive,* addressed in his oeuvre the aftermath of the Spanish Civil War and typified the literary style called *tremendismo.* He received the Nobel Prize in Literature in 1989. His *Diccionario* is a sumptuous endeavor to remedy *el pudor castizo,* the ancestral public reservations about sexual activities on the Iberian Peninsula. Like Dr. Johnson's *A Dictionary of the English Language,* it's a playful artifact, less a scientific lexicon than what Graham Greene once called "an entertainment." With a vast erudition on language and literature, Cela makes a compendium of innuendos, including such terms as *cojonudo, espermatoizómetro, huevón, monorquía, orquicatábasis, pompis, porra, redaños,* and *tompiate,* all of them difficult, if not impossible, to render in English. He also anthologizes bits and pieces of Spanish lore—mainly poetry—about sexual encounters.

In volume 1, for example, under the word *morrión,* which he elegantly defines as "tropo de intención festiva buscada en la consonancia—cojón," a word game making reference to the testicles, he has a very raunchy quote from Félix María de Samaniego's poem *La peregrinación:*

Diez árabes salieron del desierto
y en el ancho camino
cogen al matrimonio peregrino:
sin detención los dejan en pelota,
y viendo la beldad de la devota
resuelven, sin oír sus peticiones,
en su esponja limpiarse los morriones.

[From the desert came ten Arabs
and on the sand so smooth and supple
they pounced on the wandering couple:
without a thought they stripped them bare,
and seeing that beauty oh so fair,
they ignored her pleading calls
and on her sponge they wiped their balls.]

VA : Having been raised in Mexico, we were both taught
Samaniego in elementary school as the Spanish—well,
Basque, actually—answer to Aesop.

IS : His fables were supposed to turn mischievous children into
model citizens. But Samaniego, who founded the Real Semi-
nario Patriótico Bascongado and who died in 1801 at the age of
fifty-six, also had a vulgar vein. He published a collection of
libertine stories, "El jardín de Venus." The tension between
the pious and the vulgar in Samaniego's work is exactly what
Cela is after: the dirty mind, chaste on the surface, lustful on
the inside, quietly waiting for an opportunity to let the instinct
go loose. Carpe diem.

VA : It looks as though the ten Arabs seized the day. By the way,
what is the origin of the term *carpe diem?*

IS : It appears for the first time in Horace's *Carmina,* written in
the first century BCE: "Dum loquimur, fugerit invida aetas:
carpe diem, quam minimum credula postero" (book 1, ode 11).
It's generally rendered as "seize the day," but the possibility exists that Horace is making a reference to sexuality—fornication,
in particular. I assume this would come as a surprise to the
valedictorians who invoke *carpe diem* as an invitation to take
life at its fullest only in the philosophical sense.

VA : Language is metaphorical when it comes to expressions
of love.

IS : Borges once said that censorship is the mother of metaphor.

VA : Let's talk about declarations of love.

IS : The three English words *I love you* are life-transforming. A person remembers exactly when they were uttered: the time, the place, the weather . . .

VA : That, in turn, makes me think of *piropo,* a ubiquitous word in the Spanish-speaking world.

IS : The Internet is replete with sites about piropos. The word comes from the Latin *pyrōpus,* and from the Greek πυρωπός (πυρο-, fire, and -ωπός, appearance). One of its meanings in Spanish is *lisonja, requiebro.* In English, the equivalent is a flirtatious, flattering comment. In Portuguese it might be *cumprimento* and in Hungarian *bók,* but these terms can be applied to any complimentary remark, not necessarily a flirtatious one.

VA : Let's talk about terms of endearment.

IS : Such terms are also called *hypocorisms,* from the Greek *up-okore.* The word *kore* means child, and the verb *korizo* means to pamper: to pamper the child. It's interesting to note that in languages other than English, the grammatical gender of the term of endearment often does not match that of the person addressed. Since such terms have different nuances in every language, translating them is most difficult. There's an infinite number of hypocoristic terms: anybody can invent a new word or attribute a new affectionate meaning to an existing word. A partial and arbitrary list (culled from the *OED*) includes angel-puss, apricot, baby-doll, big-daddy-yum-yum, bugsy, bump-kin, Casanova, chickabiddy, cutie-patootie, dahlin, doll-face, dreamboat, dumpling, Esquire, fetcher, goodlooker, honey-bunny, hottie, inamorato, knight-in-shining-armor, kool-aid, lambey-pie, lambkin, lothario, lover-boy, muffin, munchkin, muppet, patootie, poopsy-woopsy, puddlepooper, pumpkin, rag-beggar, romeo, schatzi, sheik, shmoopsie-poo, shnoodle-bum, slick-chick, snicker-doodle, snookums, tootsie-pie, twinkles, and winky-dink.

VA : What are some terms of endearment in Hebrew?

IS : In Hebrew *janupá* and *janifá* described comments designed to please, and *divrei jizur* is a saying used during courtship. Yiddish uses a Hebraism: *janífele.* But courtship is a game, an engagement in miscommunication. What do women want to hear? Is it the same as what men want to say? Is there a gender divide? To what extent are the expressions we use to make others fall for us a map of our own obsessions? In her book *You Just Don't Understand: Women and Men in Conversation,* published in 1990, Deborah Tannen explores the fundamental divide between male and female speech. At its core, what we say to one another, she believes, is based on our own biological limitations. A *janifá,* then, is not what someone of the opposite sex wants to hear from me in the act of courtship but what I believe she wants to hear. The difference is a fundamental one. It announces that we're all prisoners of ourselves.

VA : Where does the word *courtship* come from?

IS : *Webster's* defines it as "the act of paying court, with the intent to solicit a favor," "the act of wooing in love," and the "solicitation of woman to marriage." Equally important is the word's reference to *court,* a group of legislators in charge of defining the political and judicial aspects of a society. And in the historical sense the court was the entourage—the courtiers—that surrounded monarchs and other rulers. All these meanings are connected.

The *courtier,* as defined in the dialogues in Baldassare Castiglione's *The Book of the Courtier,* written in 1528, is a well-composed individual with a universal—which, at the time, meant European—education, good manners, and a good voice. There was a craft to being a courtier, and, consequently, courtly love in the sixteenth century was understood as being shaped within the confines of those conventions. In French, dating from the late eleventh century, such love was known as *fin amour,* and in Provençal, the language par excellence of troubadour poetry, as *fin 'amors.* Let's keep in mind that Provençe from the eleventh to the thirteenth century was a laboratory of language and culture. Its impact on modern Spanish, Portuguese, and, of course, French, is unquestionable.

VA : The word *finesse* comes to mind.

IS : Speaking with finesse (in Spanish, *fineza)* is paying compliments, using one's gift of gab. Those compliments need to conform to the standards of the period. Sor Juana Inés de la Cruz, a most provocative seventeenth-century Mexican nun and my favorite Latin American poet, wrote much about the topic in her "Athenagoric Letter," relating it to Jesus Christ's finezas; or rather, she circled around it, for that's what one does with finezas, which are all about refinement and delicacy of performance, about having proper responses to particular circumstances. That's also where courting comes from today: a conventional stratagem to make one's target of affection fall in love.

For all these reasons, courtly love is infinitely baroque. Consider Sor Juana's Sonnet 165, translated by Margaret Sayers Peden:

Stay, shadow of contentment too short-lived,
illusion of enchantment I most prize,
fair image for whom happily I die,
sweet fiction for whom painfully I live.

If answering your charms' imperative,
complaint, I like steel to magnet fly,
by what logic do you flatter and entice,
only to flee, a taunting fugitive?

'Tis no triumph that you so smugly boast
that I fell victim of your tyranny;
though from encircling bonds that held you fast

your elusive form too readily slipped free,
and though to my arms you are forever lost,
you are a prisoner of my fantasy.

The shadow Sor Juana refers to is the imaginary lover trapped within the court's conventions.

The flip side of the coin is Geoffrey Chaucer's *The Miller's Tale*, which belongs to the *fabliaux*, a tradition that emerged in the Middle Ages from the literature written by the itinerant artists known in French as jongleurs. *The Miller's Tale* ridicules love and other emotions experienced by stereotypes like cuckolded husbands, abusive priests, and stupid peasants.

VA : Courtly love is about expressions of commitment, then. The literature of the jongleurs rotated around the celebration of the maiden.

IS : Yes, and the expressions used by them were overly refined to the point of circumvolution. These expressions sprang from the tradition of the troubadours, who promoted a suave new form of paganism that they called *Gai Saber*—literally, "the happy wisdom" or "gay science." By the thirteenth century, Gai Saber was institutionalized throughout Europe. Such expressions also appear in Francesco Petrarca's declarations of love to Laura, the idealized beloved who stole his heart in Sainte-Claire d'Avignon in 1327 (and who is thought by many scholars to be a fictional character). Vows of loyalty abound, as well as the idea of love as an arduous quest, as in these lines from Petrarca's sonnet "The Voyage":

I seek my double star of love in vain
Dead in the deep, both art and reason fade
And a safe harbor lies beyond my hope.

Language serves as a map for love. The emotion is too ethereal—so the understanding goes—not to be turned into an occasion to reflect on humanity as a whole. But perhaps more interesting, upon Laura's death in 1348, Petrarca wrote in his poem "To Laura in Death" that "to be able to say how much you love is to love but little." This line demonstrates how words fail even the best poets of love.

VA : Earlier on you suggested that love was Petrarca's invention. Do you mean romance?

IS : The word *romance* seems to me to be in constant mutation. We use it for courtship, to describe the emotional infatuation that accompanies physical attraction, and also to describe novels about that infatuation. In spite of what we may see in Barnes and Noble or in Hallmark stores, *romance* was originally a term that had nothing to do with love. It did not apply to a specific literary genre, either. Romance simply meant that something was either spoken or written in Romanz, the vernacular French language, which derived from the language spoken by the Romans—that is, Latin. Romanz belongs in what we currently call the Romance or Romanic languages. Starting in the late eleventh century, literature written in the vernacular was referred to as "romance" simply to distinguish it from that written in Latin, which was considered the "real" literature. It took such daring writers as Dante in Italy or Alfonso X "The Wise" in Spain to leave Latin behind and cement these emerging Romance languages as legitimate. To paraphrase Max Weinreich, these new languages started assembling an army and a navy. Gradually, the term *romance,* especially in France, Spain, and Anglo-Norman England, came to be identified with a specific kind of narrative: chivalric adventures, including Arthurian literature, the *Amadís de Gaula,* the *Chanson de Roland, Tirant lo Blanc,* the *Cantar de Mío Cid,* and so on.

The audience of the early Romance narratives was female: the queen and her feminine entourage composed of noble ladies and ladies-in-waiting. These women were interested in stories where women played a more central role. Let's not forget that poets lived off audiences they pleased, so although fighting and male bonding played a part in Romance literature, the "macho thing" was downplayed in order to please the poets' female patrons. The knights in Romance literature were motivated by love for their ladies. The knight serves his courtly lady (a duty called "love service") with the same obedience as he does his lord. The knight's love inspires him to perform great deeds. In these romances, the lady is in complete control of the love relationship.

VA: When was the term *courtly love* first coined?

IS: The term *amour courtois* was coined by a French medievalist by the name of Gaston Paris in 1883. But it was Marie de Champagne, daughter of Eleanor of Aquitaine and mother of Queen Blanche of Castile, who seven hundred years before commissioned the cleric Andreas Capellanus to codify the concept.

VA: If one considers *amor hablado,* spoken love, as well as *amor escrito,* written love, it might also be interesting to consider undeclared love. In other words, I want to talk about love that isn't expressed. Is it still love?

I S : At first your question invoked to me the tree that falls in the forest—if no one hears it, does it still make a sound? But unexpressed love does exist, of course. The idea is related to the discussion of sublimation. Let me reverse the question: What if love is strongly felt but cannot be verbally expressed? Does the emotive aspect of love inevitably seep out into other forms of expression when it cannot be spoken of? How is love affected by the prohibition of verbal expression? Can love ever be codified without speech as its medium? And what about shyness? A person might be in love with someone else but be so timid as to become mute. Of course, it's essential to remember that the act of articulating our feelings of love isn't universal. Studies have been done about verbal expressions during coitus in different cultures. Japanese women, for instance, seldom utter a word.

V A : In talking about your French lover Brigitte, you said that love and literature are connected. Let's focus on the interface between love and poetry.

I S : In *The Double Flame,* Octavio Paz claims, in Helen Lane's translation, that love "is a poetry of the body" and poetry "an eroticism of language." He adds, "They are in complementary opposition. Language—sound that carries meanings, a material trace that denotes nonmaterial things—is able to give a name to what is most fleeting and evanescent: sensation. Nor is eroticism mere animal sexuality; it's ceremony, representation. The agent that provokes both the erotic act and the poetic act is imagination. Imagination turns sex into ceremony and rite, language into rhythm and metaphor." In my view, lyric poetry, from Sappho and Catullus onward, is far more effective in defining love than lexicons are.

VA : Can you give an example?

IS : Ovid might well be the most famous poet of—and in—love. *Ars amatoria* is a delightful manual. I'm especially fond of his "Elegy #5," rendered into English by the treacherous Christopher Marlowe:

In summer's heat and mid-time of the day
To rest my limbs upon a bed I lay,
One window shut, the other open stood,
Which gave such light, as twinkles in a wood,
Like twilight glimpse at setting of the sun,
Or night being past, and yet not day begun.
Such light to shamefast maidens must be shown,
Where they may stop, and seem to be unknown.
Then came Corinna in a long, loose gown,
Her white neck hid with tresses hanging down:
Resembling fair Semiramis going to bed,
Or Lais of a thousand wooers sped.
I snatched her gown, being thin the harm was small,
Yet strived she to be covered therewithal.
And, striving thus as one that would be chaste,
Betrayed herself, and yielded at the last.
Stark naked as she stood before mine eye,
Not one wen in her body could I spy.

What arms and shoulders did I touch and see?
How apt her breasts were to be pressed to me?
How smooth a belly under her waist saw I?
How large a leg, and what a lusty thigh?
To leave the rest, all like me passing well;
I clinged her naked body, down she fell.
Judge you the rest. Being tired she bade me kiss,
Jove send me more such afternoons as this.

Ovid leaves it to the reader to imagine love in its full potential:
"Judge you the rest."

The Middle Ages modeled the form of poetic love. The tradition of the troubadour played an essential role in the making
of courtly love. The poetic tradition was shaped during the
Middle Ages in Provençe, in the form of ballads addressing a
fixation with a married lover. The songs followed a strict pattern, and the chivalric component was clear-cut. The themes
were war, politics, love, and nature. The troubadour was a
male poet carrying his emotions around. (The etymology of
the word *troubadour* is uncertain, with some linguists claiming
it comes from the Arabic verb meaning "to sing" while others
point to the Occitan language as well as to vulgar Latin, suggesting that the word describes a song composed in tropes.)
As the tradition evolved, the troubadours compiled their songs
into written collections, *chansonniers,* in which one can ana-
lyze various themes. Among the famous troubadors are Bernart
de Ventadorn, Folquet de Marseille, and Jaufré Rudel de Blaia.

The troubadours were members of the upper class. They were kings, archbishops, noblemen, and knights, including Richard the Lionheart and Alfonso X "The Wise," who was king of Castile and León. The poems were in *langue d'oc,* a predecessor of the Occitan language. The tradition spread to Germany, Italy, Spain, and other parts of France. Born into the lower social strata, these were entertainers who performed the troubadour songs and sometimes composed them as well. A number of spin-offs are traceable. In Spain and eventually in the Americas, the genre of the *pastorela* is a direct descendant of the troubadour songs, as is the *corrido,* a ballad about a heroic figure or event whose value is preserved in memory.

The love poems of the troubadours are the ones that interest me. What image of love do they project? The story of the affair between Abelard and Heloise is a decisive moment in Western views on love. It survives in epistolary form. Also, it's symptomatic that an extra autobiographical account written by Abelard is called *Historia calamitum* (The Story of My Calamities). Abelard was a thirty-eight-year-old scholar in Paris who in 1115 became the tutor of Heloise, the eighteen-year-old niece of the city's canon. Passion ignited, and Heloise became pregnant. Abelard took her to Brittany and wanted her to marry him, but she refused because the marriage would hurt his reputation. Finally, she consented, and they returned to Paris, where a secret ceremony took place. But Heloise's uncle was furious. Heloise was sent to a convent where she took her vows, and Abelard was attacked by a gang and castrated. It was thought that only eight letters between them had survived, but another pack of correspondence emerged recently. It's important to keep in mind that Abelard was a famous theologian. The eloquence in his letters is the result of deep, learned explorations of the tension between reason and passion. And Heloise, a stellar student, wasn't an innocent victim. Her religious conviction—she became an abbess—and her unremitting love for Abelard come across as the opposing forces defining women at the time. Paz argues in *The Double Flame,* "His greatest calamity was also his greatest happiness: to have met Heloise and been loved by her. Because of her he was a man: he knew love. And because of her he ceased to be a man: they castrated him."

Alexander Pope wrote a lengthy poem in 1716, titled "Eloisa to Abelard," in which he imagined Heloise, in her prison, reflecting on her affair with Abelard. It's an homage to Ovid's *Heroides,* told from the female viewpoint after the separation has occurred. Here is one of the middle stanzas:

Thou know'st how guiltless first I met thy flame,
When Love approach'd me under Friendship's name;
My fancy form'd thee of Angelic kind,
Some emanation of th' all-beauteous Mind.
Those smiling eyes, attemp'ring ev'ry ray,
Shone sweetly lambent with celestial day:
Guiltless I gaz'd; heav'n listen'd while you sung;
And truths divine came mended from that tongue.

From lips like those what precept fail'd to move?
Too soon they taught me 'twas no sin to love:
Back thro' the paths of pleasing sense I ran,
Nor wish'd an Angel whom I lov'd a Man.
Dim and remote the joys of saints I see;
Nor envy them that heav'n I lose for thee.

The poem concludes with Pope's insertion of his own role
as poet:

And sure if fate some future bard shall join
In sad similitude of griefs to mine,
Condemn'd whole years in absence to deplore,
And image charms he must behold no more;
Such if there be, who loves so long, so well;
Let him our sad, our tender story tell;
The well-sung woes will sooth my pensive ghost;
He best can paint 'em, who shall feel 'em most.

Among the proponents of courtly love was Andreas Capellanus, the twelfth-century cleric commissioned by Marie de
Champagne. In his treatise *De amore,* written in 1184–1186
and known in English as *The Art of Courtly Love,* he claims
that *love (amor)* is derived from the word *hook (amar),* which
signifies capturing or being captured: "For he who loves is
caught in the chains of desire and wishes to catch another with
his hook. Just as a shrewd fisherman tries to attract fish with

his bait and to catch them with his curved hook, so he who is truly captured by love tries to attract another with his blandishments and with all his power tries to hold two hearts together with one spiritual chain or, if they be already united, to hold them always together." Capellanus offers a series of rules of love. For example, "he who is not jealous cannot love," "love always departs from the dwelling place of avarice," "he who is vexed by the thoughts of love eats little and seldom sleeps," and "every action of a lover ends in the thought of his beloved."

v a : And then there is Shakespeare.

i s : Shakespeare is the most important of them all. In the quest to articulate the *mare magnum* that is love in Western civilization, he's in command. As Helena states in *All's Well That Ends Well,* "The hind that would be mated by the lion / Must die for love" (1.1.91–92). And in *Hamlet,* Polonius, quoting from Hamlet's letter to Ophelia, announces:

Doubt thou the stars are fine,
Doubt that the sun doth move,
Doubt truth to be a liar,
But never doubt I love. (2.2.116–119)

Yet in *Julius Caesar,* Brutus says to Lucilius:

When love begins to sicken and decay,
It useth an enforcèd ceremony.
There are no tricks in plain and simple faith. (4.2.20–22)

One of the most intriguing poems on love is Shakespeare's
Sonnet 130, part of the so-called second cycle of the Bard's
sonnets, the ones addressing not the young man but the Dark
Lady, the mysterious lover whose modes infatuate the poet
even though she's disloyal, untruthful, and promiscuous. Her
powers are earthly, imperfect, human—yet incandescent. The
poet offers a lyrical definition of love as infatuation, love as
sublime emotion, but also love as recognition of the loved
one's failings.

My mistress' eyes are nothing like the sun;
Coral is far more red than her lips' red;
If snow be white, why then her breasts are dun;
If hairs be wires, black wires grow on her head.

I have seen roses damasked, red and white,
But no such roses see I in her cheeks;
And in some perfumes is there more delight
Than in the breath that from my mistress reeks.

I love to hear her speak, yet well I know
That music hath a far more pleasing sound.
I grant I never saw a goddess go;

My mistress, when she walks, treads on the ground.
And yet, by heaven, I think my love as rare
As any she belied with false compare.

Shakespeare's poem is a parody of Petrarca's sonnets. Indeed, it's a direct response to an anonymous sonnet that circulated in England at the time, in which the mistress's eyes are compared to the sun, her lips to coral. In any case, no lexicon comes remotely as close to expressing what love is—its subterfuges, its importunities, its delights—as poems do. This is because metaphor is love's niche. Western civilization has made it its duty to talk about love obliquely, through indirect language. In Shakespeare's sonnet, the never-ending question, for starters, concerns the mistress's identity: Who was the so-called black lady? Biographical information on the Bard is scarce, let alone on his mistress—and he probably would have wanted it that way. She appears in Sonnets 127 to 154. She isn't quite as beautiful as the traditional object of adoration in Petrarchan lyricism (her breasts are dun, her hair is made of wire, she treads on the ground), and, as is attested in other poems, she loves other men. Shakespeare's language is incantatory yet indirect. Rather than showing us how she looks, he uses other objects (flowers, perfumes, and so on) to depict her. This is the style we've grown used to: evasive, ambiguous. Even the poet himself recognizes this approach at the end, announcing that his mistress "belies with false compare."

It has been said that Shakespeare's era might be seen as fundamentalist when approached from a modern perspective. Sex was limited to married couples. Any sexual encounter outside these boundaries, including sodomy, was a punishable offense. (Shakespeare's son-in-law Thomas Quiney was caught

fornicating in public in 1616 and was prosecuted for "incontinence.") Still, the English mores of the time, like ours, were
hypocritical. Prostitution was rampant, punishment for extramarital affairs and even sodomy uncommon. Shakespeare's
plays often feature bastards and prostitutes. What interests
people are the subtle ways in which Shakespeare portrays
sexuality—as libido but also as identity—in his characters.

VA : Like in *Romeo and Juliet,* for instance.

I S : *Romeo and Juliet,* as everyone knows, is about the impossibility of love by two infatuated adolescents. At its heart is the ancestral tension between the two families, the Capulets and the
Montagues. But we can also look at how the characters are
defined—is it by their sexual or their spiritual attraction? How
is love consummated? And in addition to the romance of the
main characters, there's the sexuality of Mercutio—is he gay?
The play was probably written in 1595, in what is known as the
Bard's lyrical period (he also composed *Richard II* and *A Midsummer Night's Dream* during this time). Literary historians
have long debated the exact date, with some suggesting it
could have been written anytime after 1593 and before 1597,
the latter being the year in which it first appeared in an unlicensed quarto edition. (The second quarto, which appeared
in 1599, used as its title *The Most Excellent and Lamentable
Tragedy of Romeo and Juliet.*) But there's the Nurse's remark
(1.3.25) that " 'Tis since the earthquake now eleven years,"
in reference to the London earthquake of 1584.

As for the hurdle the lovers must clear, the fight between

families is tribal. On the one hand, it recalls the confines of exogamy: you cannot mate within your group, but you cannot mate with the enemy either. On the other hand, it's about the clash between individual and social wills. Romeo and Juliet relate to one another as free souls. They pay no attention to the prohibition that defines them.

VA: The play is set in Italy, in the Veneto.

IS: Yes, right at the border with Lombardy, in Verona. The setting is an important point, given that Shakespeare (like Queen Elizabeth I) never left England. Historians know a bit of his whereabouts between Stratford-on-Avon and London, but it appears that he went hardly anywhere else. Yet he set *Hamlet* in Denmark, *The Merchant of Venice* in, well, Venice. There are also the far-flung settings of *Titus Andronicus, The Tempest,* and so on. Such choices beg the question: Does an author need to be personally acquainted with the place where his plot develops? Not necessarily. In the case of *Romeo and Juliet,* the connection to Italy is designed to invoke a cultural referent in the audience's mind: Petrarca. Indeed, the play is filled with sonnets in the Italian style. And Mercutio says of Romeo: "Now is he for the numbers that Petrarch flowed in" (2.4.36–37). In the English mind, it's a romantic locus, a landscape of innocence and discovery.

VA: Is it the greatest love story ever told?

IS: I'm struck by the "ever told" in that question. In telling stories, humans make sense of the confusion that inhabits them. And love is truly a confusing emotion. But the act of telling a story is also a device to appropriate it. From ballet to opera to literature to film, the variations of *Romeo and Juliet* are infinite. Think of Leonard Bernstein's Broadway musical *West Side Story,* set against the backdrop of ethnic tension in a New York neighborhood. The Capulets and the Montagues become the Jets and the Sharks—that is, the Italians and the Puerto Ricans. Or is it vice versa? Think of Franco Zeffirelli's 1968 film adaptation, or the 1996 Hollywood version, *William Shakespeare's Romeo + Juliet,* with Leonardo DiCaprio and Claire Danes. Each of these renditions appropriates the story of Romeo and Juliet, offering a different perspective. And there have been endless reflections on the play, including the writings of, to name a few, Samuel Taylor Coleridge, Samuel Johnson, John Dryden, Harold Bloom, and Stephen Greenblatt.

v a : How do these interpretations vary?

i s : The Romantics, for instance, focused on the aspect of ideal love in the play. Some commentators have concentrated on individual freedom against social constraints. Others have wondered if the play is truly tragic. In Greek drama, the tragic hero is the one tested by gods and circumstance. But are Romeo and Juliet tragic as a result of their character flaws?

v a : No.

i s : Right. Their tragedy comes from their environment. Contemporary views of Shakespeare's play focus more on the tension between families and sexuality, as well as on the language.

v a : We can also look at this play as a representation of the tension between Eros and Thanatos. Moving away from the stage, how is the tension between Eros and Thanatos represented in poetry?

I S : It often takes the form of a cult of death. Think of Elizabeth Barrett Browning's Sonnet 43:

How do I love thee? Let me count the ways.
I love thee to the depth and breadth and height
My soul can reach, when feeling out of sight
For the ends of being and ideal Grace.
I love thee to the level of everyday's
Most quiet need, by sun and candle-light.
I love thee freely, as men strive for Right;
I love thee purely, as they turn from Praise.
I love thee with the passion put to use
In my old griefs, and with my childhood's faith.
I love thee with a love I seemed to lose
With my lost saints—I love thee with the breath,
Smiles, tears, of all my life!—and, if God choose,
I shall but love thee better after death.

This is one of the most famous love poems in the English language, in particular the first line. Browning, the daughter of a plantation owner in England, wrote *Sonnets from the Portuguese,* the collection in which this sonnet appears, about Robert Browning, whom she ultimately married in 1846, despite her father's objections. Believing the collection to be too personal, she decided to disguise her own story by suggesting that the pieces were translations. She originally chose the title *Sonnets from the Bosnian* but eventually settled on a title inspired by her husband's affectionate pet name for her, "my little Portuguese." In Sonnet 43, Browning expresses her love in every dimension—"the depth and breadth and height"—freely, purely, and with passion. Yet the last line leaves the reader struck: "if God choose, / I shall but love thee better after death." Are we able to love thee better after death? What kind of fate are we allowed in connection with love after life?

v a : Other literary genres address this tension, too.

i s : There are a handful of mesmerizing literary explorations about love and death—different kinds of love that communicate with the beyond. Isn't Edgar Lee Master's *Spoon River Anthology* one of them? How about Juan Rulfo's *Pedro Páramo?* But I prefer briefer, more subtle items, like Ambrose Bierce's "An Occurrence at Owl Creek Bridge," written in 1886 and part of *Tales of Soldiers and Civilians,* as well as Borges's "The Secret Miracle," originally published in 1944 and first collected in English in *Labyrinth.* In both of these examples, as the respective protoganists approach death, they are allowed extra time to revisit their actions and legacy.

v a : You pay homage to "The Secret Miracle" in your Spanish-language book *Prontuario.*

i s : More than paying homage, I decided to rewrite it. I've spent hours thinking about Borges's tale, discussing it with friends, colleagues, and students. The protagonist, Jaromir Hladik,

John William Waterhouse, *Echo and Narcissus* (1903).
Oil on canvas, 43 × 74½ in. (109.2 × 189.2 cm).
© Walker Art Gallery, National Museums Liverpool.

Diego Velázquez, *La Venus del espejo* (1644).
Oil on canvas, 48⅕ × 69½ in. (122.5 × 177 cm).
Presented by the National Art Collections Fund, 1906.
© The National Gallery, London.

Diego Velázquez, *Las meninas* (1656).
Oil on canvas, 125⅕ × 108⁷⁄₁₀ in. (318 × 276 cm).
© Museo Nacional del Prado, Madrid.

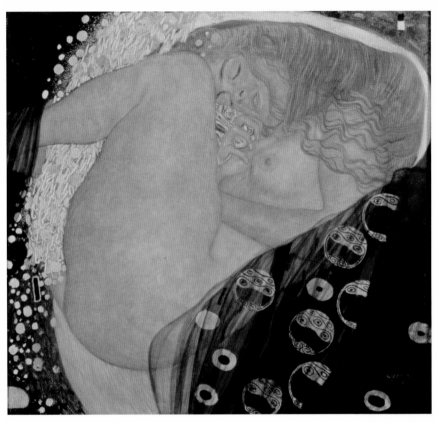

Gustav Klimt, *Danaë* (1907).
Oil on canvas, $30\frac{3}{10} \times 32\frac{7}{10}$ in. (77 × 83 cm).
The Bridgeman Art Library/Getty Images.

Joel Peter Witkin, *Las Meninas (Self Portrait)* (1987).
Toned gelatin silver photograph, 14½ × 14¾ in. (36.8 × 37.5 cm).
Collection of the Museum of Fine Arts, New Mexico.

Jan van Eyck, *Portrait of Giovanni Arnolfini and His Wife* (1434).
Oil on oak, 32⅕ × 23⅗ in. (82.2 × 60 cm). Bought, 1842.
© The National Gallery, London.

Grant Wood, *American Gothic* (1930).
Oil on beaver board, $30^{11}/_{16} \times 25^{11}/_{16}$ in. (78 × 65.3 cm) unframed.
Friends of the American Art Collection [1930.934], The Art Institute of Chicago.
Photography © The Art Institute of Chicago.

Pierre-Auguste Renoir, *Le déjeuner des canotiers* (1881).
Oil on canvas, 51¼ x 69⅛ in. (130.2 x 175.6 cm).
The Phillips Collection, Washington, D.C.

rewrites his play, though only in his mind, and then he dies. The title describes this "miracle" with the adjective *secret*. But is it possible for a miracle to be secret? Miracles are, by definition, public performances in which the cycle of Nature is interrupted. This inconsistency bothered me to the extreme, so I decided to fix it. My rewriting of Borges's piece quietly changes a series of grammatical signs and, more significantly, adds a sentence at the end.

VA : Is that plagiarism?

IS : Plagiarism is theft. My story "Otro milagro secreto" is a conscious redesign. In any case, another mesmerizing story about death—a ghost story, perhaps—is Isaac Bashevis Singer's "A Wedding in Brownsville," published in *Commentary* magazine in 1962 and later as part of his book *Old Love*. Unlike Bierce's and Borges's pieces, this one is a love story. The protagonist is a successful, mature Jewish doctor in Manhattan who has reluctantly agreed to attend the wedding of an old acquaintance's daughter. Traveling to the wedding by taxi during a snow storm, he suddenly realizes he's dead. Or is he? His arrival at the wedding is described in a confused fashion. Most people he meets at the party were killed by the Nazis in Auschwitz. How can they be alive now? Then the doctor meets his adolescent love, Rivkah, whom he also thought was long dead. They talk, and he's ready to give up everything to be with her.

In Thomas Pynchon's novel *Vineland*, the characters known as Thanatoids live life as if they were dead. It might be a stretch, but one could say that a number of authors, in their literature, have made an effort to be Thanatoids. Edgar Allan Poe is an honorary member. His poem "Annabel Lee" is an example. An even better example might be the *Narrative of Arthur Gordon Pym of Nantucket,* in particular the dreamlike sections on the hollow earth, which to me seem ghostlike. A poem by Poe I especially like is "To One in Paradise":

Thou wast that all to me, love,
For which my soul did pine—
A green isle in the sea, love,
A fountain and a shrine,
All wreathed with fairy fruits and flowers,
And all the flowers were mine.

Ah, dream too bright to last!
Ah, starry Hope! That didst arise
But to be overcast!
A voice from out the Future cries,
"On! On!"—but o'er the Past
(Dim gulf!) my spirit hovering lies
Mute, motionless, aghast!

For, alas! alas! with me,
The light of Life is o'er!
"No more—no more—no more—"
(Such language holds the solemn sea
To the sands upon the shore)

Shall bloom the thunder-blasted tree,
Or the stricken eagle soar!

And all my days are trances,
And all my nightly dreams
Are where thy grey eye glances,
And where thy footstep gleams—
In what ethereal dances,
By what eternal streams.

Poe's second-rate follower, H. P. Lovecraft, the author of such
works as *The Call of Cthulhu and Other Weird Stories* and *At
the Mountains of Madness,* is also a Thanatoid.

VA : The poems you've referred to mostly come from the English-
speaking canon. What about Latin American writers?

IS : I've already mentioned Sor Juana Inés de la Cruz. She explored love within the confines of the seventeenth-century
viceroyalty in Mexico. As an illegitimate child, she spent her
life finding a space for herself in a society in which women had
three options in life: marriage, the court, or the convent. She
became a protégée of the Vicereine María Luisa de Laguna,
countess of Paredes, with whom she might have engaged in a
lesbian affair, as speculated in *I, the Worst of All,* a film by the
late Argentine director María Luisa Bemberg. She then left the
court and became a nun—and, arguably, the best baroque poet
of the Americas during the colonial period. Her poems are
about love as a game of mirrors.

Before her, there were Quechuan, Mayan, and other aboriginal poets who reflected on physical infatuation and ecstatic emotion. Miguel León Portilla, along with Earl Shorris, edited an inviting anthology, *In the Language of Kings,* that showcases the best non-Spanish-language voices of Latin America from the sixteenth century to the present. And Ángel María Garibay, a priest and philologist who died in 1967, devoted part of his career to compiling Nahua poetry, especially the erotic kind.

VA : The Spaniards eliminated all references to eroticism in the pre-Columbian poetry they came across.

IS : They sublimated it through their Catholicism. The word to describe the Spaniards' weltanschauung is *casticismo.* The word—why not?—could be construed as an allusion to the caste system in the colonial period. But its scope is more ambitious: it describes a culture of discrete and rigid sexual mores.

VA : When did eroticism make a comeback in the region?

IS : At the end of the nineteenth century, eroticism became a feature of artistic life in Hispanic America with the *modernista* movement, which swept the region from approximately 1885 to 1915, a year before one of its leaders, the globe-trotting Nicaraguan Rubén Darío, passed away. This period coincides with the expansion of capitalism and the rise of the bourgeoisie. It's also concurrent with the expansion of urban life. Although envious of the high-brow culture attainable in Paris, the modernistas (Darío, José Martí, Julián del Casal, Manuel Gutiérrez Nájera, José Asunción Silva, Amado Nervo, José

Santos Chocano, and Leopoldo Lugones, among others) began, finally, to appreciate their metropolitan centers as worthy habitats for the poet as creator. Also, just as Coleridge was infatuated with the Orient, they were hypnotized by symbols and motifs from China, India, Japan, and Africa, finding in them a type of mystery largely unattainable in their immediate surroundings, although some of them did focus on Africans in the Americas as emblems of primitivism. What is more, they delved into eroticism—largely because the Romantics in Europe were also interested in the topic—in a way previously unimaginable in the Hispanic world.

VA : What are some important examples?

IS : Delmira Agustini, a woman of renown among the modernistas in Hispanic America, wrote erotic poetry that was quite scandalous for her time. A Uruguayan born in 1886, Agustini—called "La nena" by family and friends—was a member of the Montevideo upper class, but her life was filled with melodrama. She had a passion for poetry and, it appears, an ardent desire to explore love within and beyond the conventions of the time. After a long courtship, she married a man with little interest in art. A couple of months after the marriage, however, she returned to her parents' home and filed for divorce. She then began a secret correspondence with her husband, as if their relationship were illicit. She also engaged in an amorous exchange with another man, the Argentine writer Miguel Ugarte. Her ex-husband found out about her duplicity, and during one of their secret encounters he fired two bullets at her, killing her immediately, then turned the gun on himself and committed suicide.

Agustini's poem "Fiera de amor," part of the book *Los cálices vacíos* (1913), which included a portico by Darío, is among the most sexually risqué ever to appear in Spanish. Her work doesn't really compare to anything else composed by the modernistas with the exception perhaps of Darío's "La bailarina de los pies desnudos" and "La negra Dominga." The following lines are from an English translation of "La negra Dominga" by Greg Simon and Steven F. White:

Have any of you met black Dominga,
that cross between *cafre* and *mandinga?*
She's an ebony bloom looking for bliss.
She adores ochre colors, red and green.
She is the best nibbler you've ever seen,
and all she yearns for is a Spaniard's kiss.

Like a passionate serpent that's on fire,
she's the honey and pepper of desire.
She's crazy with passion. Don't be misled:
she's the fiery lover Venus praised,
and the Queen of Sheba wished she'd saved
for King Solomon and their nights in bed.

Triumphant, fierce, and proud in her grandeur
with a stalking panther's feline allure . . .

she flashes her teeth like coconut meat,
reflecting an ivory, milky light.

v a : What about Alfonsina Storni?

i s : Storni, a representative of the postmodernist movement, is
another example of *amor fatal.* The Swiss-born Argentinean
poetess—whose tragic suicide by drowning inspired Ariel
Ramírez and Félix Luna to compose the ode "Alfonsina y el
mar"—suffered from severe depression. She was close to
Uruguayan writer Horacio Quiroga, and his death profoundly
affected her. She also was in pain because of a frustrated love
for an intellectual she never identified. Some scholars have
speculated it was Leopoldo Lugones, yet others have named
Alfredo Palacios. Storni's poetry could be passionately erotic
as readily as sickeningly sweet and cloying.

And there's Pablo Neruda. I recently translated a poem
from his collection *The Captain's Verses,* published anony-
mously in 1952 because the author was at the time ending his
marriage to his second wife, Delia del Carril, and having an affair with Matilde Urrutia, who would become his third wife.
The poem is called "Your Laughter":

Deprive me of bread, if you want,
deprive me of air, but
don't deprive me of your laughter.

Don't deprive me of the rose,

the spear you shed the grains with,
the water splashing
swiftly in your joy,
the sudden silver wave
born in you.

My struggle is painful. As I return
with my eyes sometimes tired
for watching
the unchanging earth,
your laughter enters
and raises to heaven
in search of me,
to open
all the doors of life.

My loved one, in the darkest hour,
unsheath your laughter,
and if suddenly
you see my blood staining
the cobblestones,
laugh, for your laughter
will be for my hands
like an unsullied sword.

Near the sea in autumn,
your laughter must rise
in its cascade of foam,

and in spring, my love,
I want your laughter
to be like the flower I anticipated,
the blue flower, the rose
of my resonant homeland.

Laugh at the night,
at the day, at the moon,
laugh at the twisted
streets of the island,
laugh at this clumsy
young man who loves you.
Yet when I open my eyes
and close them,
when my steps go,
when my steps return,
deny me bread, air,
light, spring,
but never your laughter
for I would die.

It's important to add another dimension to this discussion: music. In Spanish, the songs of Julio Iglesias, Emmanuel, and Juan Gabriel rotate around love: passionate love, tormented love, unrequited love. It might be possible to map out the emotional life of Hispanic adolescents by looking at the themes of major music hits. The Argentine tango in particular is, to invoke Shakespeare, about "love's labour's lost."

VA: Let's move on to the novel—how does the novel differ from poetry?

IS: Poetry is about metaphor. It's also about concision. The novel, by contrast, is expansive and exploratory.

VA: The romance is a popular genre.

IS: In Spanish it's called *novela rosa,* pink novel. The most celebrated Spanish-language author in the tradition is Corín Tellado. Wander in your local drugstore or in an airport shop while waiting for a flight and you'll come across an endless number of romances. They are perennial bestsellers. Publishers of romance novels give authors paint-by-numbers instructions. The Harlequin Romance editorial guidelines, for instance, call for fifty thousand to fifty-five thousand words showcasing "warm and tender emotions, with no sexual implicitness; lovemaking should only take place when emotional commitment between the characters justifies it."

VA: What kind of love is explored in the novel?

IS: Love in novels is usually defined by ambivalence and dissatisfaction. Think of Tolstoy's *Anna Karenina,* with the suicidal ending, or Flaubert's *Madame Bovary.* In the small provincial town of Rouen, Emma Bovary's marriage is trite, inconsequential, and she wastes her time reading books—notice the homage to *Don Quixote*—while longing for an ingredient that will give meaning to her life. Flaubert's portrait of marriage is subtle. His protagonist internalizes her displeasure—she's quietly emotional. Flaubert once said, "A man has missed something if he has never woken up in an anonymous bed beside a face he'll never see again, and if he never left a brothel at dawn feeling like jumping off a bridge into the river out of sheer physical disgust at life."

The first modern novel is Cervantes's *Don Quixote,* a parody of chivalry literature. A fifty-year-old hidalgo, Alonso Quijano, whose name is as unstable as he himself is psychologically unfit to handle the world, spends all his time—and dries up his brain—reading *novelas de caballería.* Eventually, his world is turned upside down as his fantasy takes control of his behavior. He becomes an errant knight in search of an idealized maiden, Dulcinea del Toboso, who turns out to be none other than the average local girl, Aldonza Lorenzo. Unlike such predecessors as Chaucer's *Canterbury Tales,* there's an arch to the narrative that involves the coordinates of space and time. Furthermore, the protagonist undergoes an external and internal transformation, characteristics of what later would be described as bildungsroman. And what makes the errant knight tick? Love, love, love . . . love of books, love of justice, love for his maiden.

VA : What about love in the short-story genre?

IS : The brevity of the form allows for a compressed snapshot of the convulsions of the heart. There's an immortal story called "End of the Game," by the Argentine author Julio Cortázar, about blissful children waiting on the railway tracks for the train to pass while they pose as statues. Is it about love? I'm not sure, although in my mind—I read it years ago—it re-creates the sporadic, passionate impression of first love. Cortázar also has stories about missed encounters in the Paris Metro that linger the way failed romances do. Isaac Babel's "First Kiss," William Faulkner's "A Rose for Emily," and Anton Chekhov's "Lady with Dog" are superb examples of stories about love. Isaac Bashevis Singer left us more than 350 stories, the majority of them about love. "Yentl" is about a transsexual. Borges isn't known as a romantic, but "The Aleph," modeled after the *Divine Comedy,* with the image of Beatriz Viterbo dead at the beginning, is haunting. Thomas Hardy's "The Son's Veto" and Oscar Wilde's "The Nightingale and the Rose" are memorable.

V A : This conversation makes me think about book dedications. If you were to take at random one hundred books out of your library and read the authors' dedications, my guess is that of those where a clear relationship to the author can be established, half of them are dedicated to spouses.

I S : Book dedications are fascinating in that they're hardly disinterested. Historically, persons considered suitable for dedications were often the high and mighty who, with their good graces, might help an author keep food on the table or be spared from death. Crafting these paeans required sharp political skills. Copernicus dedicated his dangerous astronomical theory to Pope Paul III in a cleverly worded paean in hopes of earning him protection. Likewise, Thomas Paine, in his *Rights of Man,* highly critical of despotism, including that of King

George III's, dedicated his book to George Washington, trusting that King George's need for better Anglo-American relations would prevent him from going after Paine.

VA : And then there's Dr. Johnson.

IS : Few know that Johnson, often short of funds, was frequently commissioned by less-talented authors to write dedications for their books. As far as Johnson's own books are concerned, he dedicated the plan for his *Dictionary* to Lord Chesterfield, who gave him ten pounds and then ignored Johnson until the book appeared. Johnson's definition of *patron* was crafted with Chesterfield in mind.

VA : I want to return to *Dictionary Days*. At the end of the chapter "The Invention of Love," you say, "Oftentimes, the best way to find a definition in a dictionary is to simply look up the wrong word. Years ago I read the best definition for *love*. I found it in a Hallmark card: 'Love is a maelstrom.' I looked up *maelstrom* in the *OED:* 'a famous whirlpool in the Arctic Ocean on the west coast of Norway, formerly supposed to suck in and destroy all vessels within a long radius.'" Poetry does the same, you seem to imply. It uses metaphors to describe love . . .

IS : And those metaphors are the closest we get to understanding what love is. Through poetry it is far easier to understand love than through any scientific treatise. And if poets don't define it, at least they offer a syntax to appreciate it: "How do I love thee? Let me count the ways."

VA : Love articulated . . .

IS : And concealed.

IV

VA : You've talked about beauty in the work of Darwin and Leone
Ebreo. Let's explore the topic of beauty further.

IS : Beauty is a spiritual pleasure as well as an inherited value. The
OED, not surprisingly, has trouble coming up with a suitable
definition. It first describes the word as a "combined perfection of form and charm of colouring as affords keen pleasure to
the sense of sight." But upon realizing the shortcomings of
such a definition, it expands its scope by suggesting it is "that
quality or combination of qualities which affords keen pleasure to other senses (e.g., that of hearing), or which charms
the intellectual or moral faculties, through inherent grace, or
fitness to a desired end." In any case, beauty is in the eye of the
beholder, as David Hume suggested in "Of the Standard of
Taste." "Beauty is no quality in things themselves," he stated.
"It exists merely in the mind that contemplates them." And

Catullus, in the poem "Carmen 86," part of his cycle about the mysterious Lesbia, writes:

Quintia formosa est multis. mihi candida, longa,
recta est: haec ego sic singula confiteor.
totum illud formosa nego: nam nulla uenustas,
nulla in tam magno est corpore mica salis.
Lesbia formosa est, quae cum pulcherrima tota est,
tum omnibus una omnis surripuit Veneres.

Here is an English translation by Peter Green (2005):

Many find Quintia beautiful. For me she's fair-
     complexioned, tall,
of good carriage. These few points I concede.
But overall beauty—no. There's no genuine attraction
in that whole long body, not one grain of salt.
It's Lesbia who's beautiful, and, being wholly lovely,
has stolen from all of the others their every charm.

The beholder establishes the scale of appreciation and offers a value judgment. From Plato to the Enlightenment, however, the argument was made that beauty is a universal quality. In other words, through proper education, humans anywhere on the globe would agree on what's beautiful. We know better now, thanks in large part to the Romantics, who suggested that the concept of beauty varies from one individual to another.

VA: What's Plato's theory of beauty?

IS: In *The Symposium,* Plato talks of Beauty Itself, an ideal resulting from a "ladder of love." That ladder starts in the earthly and ends in the abstract. For him earthly beauty is a degradation of sorts. He prefers a higher, loftier pursuit, which animates our search for an ethereal model.

VA: And what was the prevailing theory of beauty during the Enlightenment?

IS: In the Age of Reason, the universal approach to beauty was based on natural rights. The assumption was that everyone was able to reach an advanced understanding as a result of education. Appreciating beauty was no longer the domain of the courtesans but achievable by everyone through "the cultivation of the spirit."

VA: How do we know if something is beautiful?

IS: Empirically. It comes from perception. The appreciation of harmony—color, sound, taste—comes from shared experience and is the result of maturity. A three-year-old child doesn't understand beauty unless and until an adult points it out. Eventually, socialization leads us to appreciate beauty in ways that are handed down by previous generations. One culture might find beauty in a Rembrandt painting of a dogfight, but another culture might recognize it as a dogfight and dislike it.

VA: Is beauty an attribute of femininity?

IS: The confines of our language force us to see it that way. A woman is beautiful whereas a man is handsome. In Western civilization, the harmony one finds in a natural scene or in a work of art is connected with an ideal of female beauty as balanced and authentic. That ideal changes with time. The concept of beauty in Rembrandt's time was based on plumpness. His work is filled with protuberant breasts and stocky waists. Our understanding is radically different. Magazines, Hollywood movies, and TV shows perpetuate a model of beauty for our time based on thinness, maybe even anorexia. The slimmer the body and the tighter the clothes, the more appealing women are thought to be. Obesity today isn't an asset but a defect. These differences are palpable from year to year, as the model is reshaped by society. In the United States in the 1940s, a Somali woman wouldn't have been considered beautiful by mainstream culture, nor would her Mexican, Pakistani, and Korean counterparts. Beauty is defined by class, ethnicity, and religion.

v a : And how does beauty connect to love?

i s : To love someone is to feel an attraction. That attraction is in part innate—each of us has a Platonic mate in our DNA—and in part defined by our context.

v a : Does anyone use the word *beauty* anymore? Its use seems to me to be declining.

i s : I think you're right; it's rarely used among adults. A certain aesthetic correctness pushes us to dismiss it as too subjective to be taken seriously.

v a : Yet beauty isn't only physical.

i s : One might say that there are two types of beauty: natural and artistic. Natural beauty isn't exclusively about what the eyes see. Pythagoras believed in the connection between beauty and numbers. In his view mathematics was about perfection, and beauty is an expression of perfection. In today's world, beauty is marketable—more so, I'm convinced, than ever before. The paradox of Plato's cave, which presents the argument that the world in which we live is only appearances and that the essence of things is to be found elsewhere, has pushed society to the manufacturing of aesthetic satisfaction. This is especially true in the United States, a civilization imbued with the concept of eternal entertainment. Look around: pleasure and relaxation are the ultimate values. You place a coin in a machine and in return you get a condom, an aspirin, a cold drink.

This drive to be satisfied is intimately linked to our appreciation of beauty. What is beautiful? That which comes close to our internalized model of perfection. In the female body, it's a set of lustful lips, an hourglass waist, and rounded breasts of the type displayed, to a dizzying degree, in women's magazines. The concept of female beauty changes as society is transformed by ethnic, religious, class, and cultural factors.

It's painful to recognize the impact of plastic surgery on the human body. The quest for perfection persuades scores of people—predominantly women—to alter their physique. Although such medical procedures are new, altering one's appearance for pride's sake or to impress a lover has been common since antiquity. The Roman poet Martial, in one of his epigrams (book 3, no. 43), states in Latin:

Mentiris iuvenem tinctis, Laetine, capillis,
tam subito corvus, qui modo cycnus eras.
Non omnes fallis; scit te Proserpina canum:
Personam capiti detrahet illa tuo.

In the English translation by Walter C. A. Car, published as
part of a multivolume effort called *Epigrammata* between 1920
and 1925:

You feign youth, Laetinus, with dyed hair
to the degree that suddenly you are a raven, but lately you
  were a swan.
You do not deceive all; Proserpina knows you are aged:
She will remove the mask from your head.

VA: Speaking of perfection and mathematics, is beauty measurable?
IS: Think of *Miss Universe,* a sorrowful legacy of the Enlightenment. The contest annually crowns "the beauty queen of the
  planet." Nations from all over the world send candidates, and a
  panel evaluates their physique, their skills, their intellectual
  ability, and so on. It's an embarrassment of kitsch, not only because it stresses that only women are beautiful but also because there's no consensus on beauty.
   Christopher Marlowe wrote a famous iambic pentameter
  poem in his *Doctor Faustus* referring to Helen of Troy that
  began, "Was this the face that launch'd a thousand ships and

burnt the topless towers of Ilium?" Helen, by the way, was not of Troy, but of Sparta. The Greeks sailed to Troy to recover Helen, who had been carried off to that land by Paris, and a war, which lasted ten years, was fought over her. All this to say that there exists an unconventional unit of measurement for beauty: the millihelen—the amount of beauty required to launch one ship.

VA : You wrote a sardonic story, "Plastic Surgery," consisting only of dialogue, in which a housewife begs her husband to give her some of his skin because her overindulgence in plastic surgery has left the doctors without a viable section of her body from which to take healthy skin in order to keep improving her looks. "¡Hazlo por amor!" she begs him. "Do it for love!"

IS : The subplot is that Judaism prohibits modifying the body. No enhancements, no transplants, no tattoos.

VA : What about earrings?

IS : Not even earrings—no piercings of any kind are allowed. Orthodox Jewish men insist that their spouses not beautify themselves in order not to become lascivious. Even natural hair is considered threatening; thus, they require their wives to shave their heads and cover themselves with a wig. And on top of the wig they use a scarf. The rationale is straightforward: women are companions to men, and their purpose in life is to bear children. Thus, eroticism is useful insofar as it results in pregnancy. The connection between my story and the attitude of Orthodox Jews is clear: beauty is natural. And nature, by definition, is erotic. To engage in plastic surgery is to embrace falsification. Likewise, to ask women to shave their hair is to turn them into reproduction machines.

The aesthetic celebration of human beauty as an attribute of nature is the outcome of Romanticism: the lover's simple qualities viewed as expressions of character. Indeed, Romanticism was a return to the principles of courtly poetry and a response to the endorsement of reason proposed by the Enlightenment. The movement took place in the late eighteenth century in France, Germany, Italy, and England. The romantic ideal is about the self, the struggle of the individual to allow emotions to reign within the social context (and sometimes beyond). The emergence of this type of sensibility, it ought to be remembered, coincided with—or should I say was integral to?—the consolidation of capitalism as a form of economic transaction. The philosophy of capitalism is free enterprise. The conviction that the individual should be the master of his own destiny, and certainly of his emotions, is essential.

Goethe's novel *Sorrows of Young Werther,* about a temperamental young man, was published in 1774. I read somewhere that as a result of the novel, a wave of suicides overwhelmed Europe at the end of the eighteenth century. The novel was seen as an endorsement of turbulent emotions. At the core of Romanticism is a misunderstood hero crying to be appreciated in his own terms. That explains why the movement is connected to the French Revolution of 1789.

One must keep in mind the number of false resonances of the word *romantic.* Today it's taken to mean, as the *OED* suggests, that which is "characterized by the subordination of form to theme, and by imagination and passion." The Oxford dons also give a second definition: "of a fabulous and fictitious character; having no foundation in fact." But we also use the word *romantic* to refer to a love scene, and we use the term with some sarcasm: the romantic scene is slightly exaggerated, more saccharine than measured. And, in terms of character, it means having a tendency to fall in love and to engage in scenes distinguishable by their emotional component.

Thus, it's important to distinguish between *romantic* and *Romantic.* The latter term is sometimes characterized by a temperament in motion, displaying extreme emotions and celebrating the individual as the center of the cosmos. In music, convulsive movements by Mozart, Haydn, and Beethoven announce the turmoil in the Romantic heart. In literature, it includes Aleksandr Pushkin with his long Russian poem *Eugene Onegin,* Goethe with *Faust,* and the English poets Lord Byron, John Keats, and Thomas Carlyle. But Romanticism is also about the bizarre and the grotesque. Mary Shelley's novel *Frankenstein; or, The Modern Prometheus,* a meditation on death and resurrection as well as a foreshadowing of what twentieth-century science sought to achieve, is the quintessential romantic novel. No wonder it's one of the bibles of contemporary science fiction. Edgar Allan Poe, often ridiculed as a second-rate writer in his native United States yet overvalued in France (thanks, in large measure, to Baudelaire), is also a Romantic, along with Ralph Waldo Emerson, whose seven lectures on representative men (including Plato, Emmanuel Swedenborg, Napoleon, and Goethe himself) are emblems of the movement in America.

VA : In talking of beauty, you've also made allusions to taste.

IS : In the discipline called aesthetics, taste is, according to the *OED,* "the faculty of discerning what is aesthetically excellent or appropriate." Again, taste is the result of socialization, which is the principal argument expounded by twentieth-century French sociologist Pierre Bourdieu, author of *Distinction: A Social Critic of the Judgment of Taste,* published in an English rendition in 1984. Taste isn't universal but acquired. It determines what's beautiful to different individuals and groups. Bourdieu developed the concept of *habitus,* which refers to the daily practices of individuals in a particular environment, a set of cognitive responses based on individual experience.

VA : Does this concept contradict the saying "there's no accounting for taste"?

IS : Yes and no. While taste is predictable, it is also subjective. Each person develops an individual taste, but within specific parameters.

VA : Taste also refers to flavor.

IS : In Spanish, *gusto.* Taste is one of the five senses. Empirically, the data it provides comes to us via the gustatory hairs, but each person's interpretation of that data is different. Does Manchego cheese taste the same to you and me? We might describe it using the same adjectives, but it is impossible to know whether we are experiencing the same thing. As the idealist philosopher Bishop Berkeley once suggested, reality might be verifiable only through perception. Berkeley's motto was *esse est percipi,* to be is to be perceived.

V A : Speaking of flavors, how do food and love go together?

I S : Food is another referent to time and place. It's an attribute of status, gender, ethnicity, and religion. Its power affects mood, and the succor one takes from it might be seen as equivalent to an orgasm, a Greek term that means "to swell with moisture." (The *OED* is at its most prudish—maybe I should say puritanical—when offering a definition: "immoderate or violent excitement of feeling." It adds, "rage, fury; a paroxysm of excitement or rage.") More than anything else, food is a sign of character. The other day I found a quote in the *Encyclopedia Britannica*—which, metaphorically, is a feast for the senses (especially its 1911 edition)—about "the psycho-physiological reaction that a well-prepared meal can have upon the human organism. The combination of various sensuous reactions— the visual satisfaction of the sight of appetizing food, the olfactory stimulation of their pleasing smells and the tactile gratification afforded the oral mechanism by rich, savory dishes— tend to bring on a state of general euphoria conducive to sexual expression."

V A : Might that state also come by invoking the words we use for food? When I say *cheese,* for instance, I feel the pungent *ees* going up my nostrils. My son, Axel, has written about these words and classified them as *synesthepoeic:* words that are perceived through the senses.

I S : There are a handful of those words, especially in French. *Mousse* makes one moan and sigh.

V A : Can we consume words?

I S : The expression "food for thought" is accurate, for words are often treated as food. People mince their words, and spit them out. A word can be a mouthful, or we can put words in somebody's mouth. We can be told to eat our words, and also to eat our hearts out.

V A : We sometimes bite off more than we can chew.

I S : Exactly. How do you like them apples? Or, in Spanish, *¡chúpate esa mandarina!* In Spanish slang, the words for *vagina*—and the derogatory *cunt*—are related to food and are plentiful: *pepa, papaya, arepa, panocha, choclo, concha, cajeta,* and *tamal.* The penis is called *camote, pepino, plátano, chile,* and *camarón.* Semen is *leche.* A handsome man is a *mango,* a *churro,* and a *bombón,* and a lover, as in Plato, is referred to as *media naranja.*

The French semiotician Roland Barthes, who died in 1980 at the age of sixty-five and was the author of *Camera Lucida* and *The Fashion System,* among other books, tasted language with the *tongue,* one might say, in both senses of the word. For him food becomes the link between body and intellect, nature and culture, wisdom and knowledge, objectivity and subjectivity. In his autobiography, Barthes compared himself to a "vigilant cook" who carefully prepares a dish—the text. In a speech at the Collège de France, he said that a good text requires "no power, a little knowledge, a little wisdom, and as much flavor as possible." Barthes wanted us to confront ourselves and to taste the flavor of words in order to obtain physical as well as intellectual pleasure, for, as he saw it, it's the flavor of words that provides knowledge. In his *Pleasure of the Text* he urges people not to devour but to graze at texts.

It's also common to describe words as fluids. Think of onomatopoeia, the naming of a thing or action by a vocal imitation of the sound associated with it: *babble, burble,* and *murmur* started out describing the sounds water makes and were then applied, by analogy, to speech. There's also *spout* and *gush,* words that originally described the movement of water but now also apply to speech. One's language is said to be fluent—from Latin *fluere,* to flow—and a conversation might be said to flow smoothly. And one should be careful not to interrupt someone's torrent of words in midstream.

VA: Continuing with the idea of food and love being intertwined, what about eating one's lover?

IS: Not even the Marquis de Sade contemplated it, but an integral part of our desire is to possess what we love. It takes the expression "hungry for love" to its extreme. In Christianity, the body of Jesus Christ is eaten in the sacramental rite. Is this a form of cannibalism? There's a film by the British director Peter Greenaway, *The Cook, the Thief, His Wife, and Her Lover,* in which cannibalism is linked to elegant cooking. Along the same lines, if also more subtle and thus more erotic, Christina Rossetti has a long poem called "Goblin Market," excerpted here:

She dropped a tear more rare than pearl,
Then sucked their fruit globes fair or red:
Sweeter than honey from the rock,
Stronger than man-rejoicing wine,
Clearer than water flowed that juice;
She never tasted such before,
How should it cloy with length of use?
She sucked and sucked and sucked the more
Fruits which that unknown orchard bore,
She sucked until her lips were sore;
Then flung the emptied rinds away,
But gathered up one kernel-stone,
And knew not was it night or day
As she turned home alone.
. . . .
She cried "Laura," up the garden,
"Did you miss me?
Come and kiss me.
Never mind my bruises,
Hug me, kiss me, suck my juices
Squeezed from goblin fruits for you,
Goblin pulp and goblin dew.
Eat me, drink me, love me;

Laura, make much of me:
For your sake I have braved the glen
And had to do with goblin merchant men."

Rossetti's line "Eat me, drink me, love me" is superb. Isn't that exactly what a lover longs for in the moment of the encounter? Metaphorically, a lover is a cannibal.

I'm also thinking of "Figs," an unrhyming poem by D. H. Lawrence, which begins with the following lines:

The proper way to eat a fig, in society,
Is to split it in four, holding it by the stump,
And open it, so that it is a glittering, rosy, moist, honied,
    heavy-petalled four-petalled flower.

Then you throw away the skin
Which is just like a four-sepalled calyx,
After you have taken off the blossom, with your lips.

But the vulgar way
Is just to put your mouth to the crack, and take out the
    flesh in one bite.

VA: Food is also at the core of social occasions.
IS: Food is sustenance—was it Dr. Johnson who said, "For a man seldom thinks with more earnestness of anything than he does

of his dinner"? And, universally, food is so frequently enjoyed with company. *Companion* comes from the Latin *com-,* with someone, and *panis,* bread. It means to break bread with someone. In *Don Juan,* Lord Byron includes these lines:

All human history attests
That happiness for man,—the hungry sinner!—
Since Eve ate apples, much depends on dinner. (canto 13,
    stanza 99)

In the Icelandic sagas food was always served, and Vikings enjoyed lavish feasts. In Henry Wadsworth Longfellow's *Song of Hiawatha,* inspired by the nineteenth-century Finnish epic poem "Kalevala," the connection between British settlers and Indians is based on food. And in Leonardo da Vinci's painting *The Last Supper,* the last moment before death is accompanied by food. The image is striking in its sobriety. The love between Jesus and his disciples is symbolized by the meal. And Christ's body, through the Eucharist, was disseminated by the Church to its followers.

Marriage in particular is often accompanied with expansive feasts. In biblical times, a wedding could take place over an entire week with food aplenty. In Matthew 22:1–14, heaven is likened to a wedding feast:

The Kingdom of Heaven is like a certain king, who made a marriage feast for his son, and sent out his servants to call

*those who were invited to the marriage feast, but they
would not come. Again he sent out other servants, saying,
"Tell those who are invited, 'Behold, I have made ready my
dinner. My oxen and my fatlings are killed, and all things
are ready. Come to the marriage feast!'"*

In Shakespeare's plays—think of *Macbeth*—feasts turn into orgies of violence. Shakespeare lived at a time when the wedding feast included such fancy dishes as peacock, lavishly prepared and served with bread and potatoes, and the staple drink of the period, ale. In *Don Quixote,* Camacho's wedding feast becomes the stage for a stolen bride. And Rabelais makes fun of the overindulgence of wedding parties.

v a : What about the wedding cake?

i s : The wedding cake is a tradition that, once again, celebrates love with bread.

v a : Do you remember that Mexican cultural icon, the Panadería Ideal?

i s : It was a veritable feast for the senses, right next to the Cine Savoy, on Avenida 16 de Septiembre. The wedding cakes displayed in its windows were monumental—maybe reaching a height of eight feet. They were tacky too, like the Taj Mahal with Arctic motifs. At the top were two stoic models (action figures?) of the bride and groom, both impeccably dressed, he in a black tuxedo, she in a white gown. I remember puzzling over how the cakes were transported to the banquet—on a tractor?

v a : Following the wedding banquet comes the honeymoon. What is the origin of *honeymoon*?

i s : I'm not sure. There are a number of theories. The word might come from the Norse *hjunottsmanathr,* which wasn't connected with a social event after the marital covenant. Instead, it related to stolen brides and to the couple's hiding to escape the authorities. Another interpretation relates to a northern European custom, in which married couples drank mead—honey wine—for a month in order to procreate a male heir.

v a : In popular culture, the feast, particularly as it is being prepared, is alluring.

i s : In cinema especially, one of my long-standing passions, the kitchen is the realm of potions and the place where human emotions converge, or else, where those emotions are manipulated. A number of movies have addressed this topic, including the Italian *La grande abbuffata;* the Japanese *Tampopo;* the Danish *Babette's Feast,* based on a story by Isak Dinesen; the Mexican *Like Water for Chocolate,* based on Laura Esquivel's novel; and the Polish *Wesele* (The Wedding), by Andrzej Wajda, based on Stanislaw Wyspianski's play. Each of these films stresses a different link between love and food. *Like Water for Chocolate* turns feminism on its head. The kitchen is portrayed as a woman's realm and, on occasion, as a laboratory of aphrodisiacs. But it isn't a place for passivity. The protagonist is able to affect people through the food she cooks. *Babette's Feast* is about cooking as a sensual art, and *La grande abuffata* is a critique of the bourgeoisie and its need to consume and control. There's also Luis Buñuel's *Discreet Charm of the Bourgeoisie,* a film made in 1972, which satirized the food-for-love tale. The power of cinema is found in the capacity of culinary images to make the audience salivate and also feel disgusted.

VA : Your story "Twins" is about siblings competing against each other through food.

IS : They eat until they die.

VA : One of the pleasures of the story is the listing of hors d'oeuvres, dishes, desserts, and so on.

IS : I'm invariably flabbergasted with the way well-to-do people talk about food, often while eating. I used to have a Cuban friend whose culinary passion was uncontrollable. I find it obscene.

VA : Let's talk about food and sin.

IS : Obviously, the fruit that symbolizes sin is the apple. Hildegard of Bingen, the medieval healer who advocated natural medicine and used plants, animals, trees, and stones to cure people, wrote that "in the fruit trees are hidden certain of God's secrets." The apple is the forbidden fruit par excellence. It's the only fruit singled out in Genesis 3:8–12, although the King James Version doesn't use the word *apple* per se: "And when Eve saw that the tree was good for food and that it was pleasant to the eye, she took the fruit thereof, and did eat, and gave also unto her husband, and he did eat. And the eyes of them both were opened, and they knew that they were naked."

The apple's suggestive colors, its feminine core if sliced

vertically, its hidden, satanic five-pointed star—the pentagram—if sliced horizontally, and the fact that when ripe it turns harder, not softer, led alchemists like Vincent de Beauvais to claim that it was a sign of the Devil, and that the apple had an immoral, cruel, and misleading nature. Its connection to love has been established ever since. But it's not necessarily mentioned as such.

VA : Why doesn't the King James Bible use the word *apple?*

IS : In biblical Hebrew the word used in Genesis is *pri haadamah,* the fruit of the earth. It isn't the word *tapuach,* apple. In folklore, the need for concreteness has given place to a change. What, after all, is "the fruit of the earth"? The Tree of Science (also known as the Tree of Life and the Tree of Knowledge of Good and Evil) is tempting because of its offering. But is it an apple tree? Not conclusively. The etymological confusion is emphasized in the Vulgate: in Latin the words for apple and evil are the same, *malum.* In various Biblical exegeses, called *midrashim,* the suggestion is made that the forbidden fruit was a grape, a fig, wheat, or citron.

Similarly, there's a distinction in the Bible between snakes and serpents. What is the difference between the two? Which one tempted Eve? In any case, the images of the apple and the snake are inseparable. The snake's phallic form led to the interpretation that Eve was tempted by Adam's penis. Likewise, there are a number of references in Greek mythology to the snake becoming an organ of penetration. According to Plutarch, Alexander the Great was born when a snake penetrated his mother, Olympias. And the apple represents the woman's breast, an object of male adoration. Interestingly, the lump at the front of the neck, known as the laryngeal protuberance, is commonly called an Adam's apple. The descendants of Noah Webster, in their 1913 edition of *Webster's Dictionary,* suggest that the term "is so called from a notion that it was caused by the forbidden fruit (an apple), sticking in the throat of our first parent." Yet men generally have a more visible laryngeal protuberance. Shouldn't it be the other way around, since Eve was the one tasting the forbidden fruit? To confound matters even more, in Spanish it is sometimes called a nut—*nuez de Adán.*

VA : How does forbidden fruit relate to the Christian sin of fornication?

IS : Saint Augustine is the architect of the Christian denial of pleasure, sexual and otherwise. In the fourth century, he articulated a doctrine of original sin that is a centerpiece of Christian theology. It suggests that Adam and Eve, by eating the forbidden fruit (that is, engaging in sexual intercourse) became corrupt. In other words, to Augustine human nature is corrupt. Only the divinity is able to redeem a sinner. But his argument against lust goes further. He believed in chastity as the road to salvation. Lust manifests itself in a person's life through permanent sexual temptation, which leads to pleasure. Physical pleasure is the opposite of chastity. In Augustine's view, sex should be about procreation only. A model individual always fought against carnal satisfaction, as he himself did according to his *Confessions.* In the book he's surprisingly eloquent when it comes to the art of sublimating love. He had been a hedonist during his youth in Carthage, where he met a woman who bore him a child. Carthage, he states at one point, "seethed all around me a cauldron of lawless loves. I loved not yet, yet I loved to love, and out of a deep-seated want, I hated myself for wanting not. I sought what I might love, in love with loving, and I hated safety. . . . To love then, and to be beloved, was sweet to me; but more, when I obtained to enjoy the person I loved. I defiled, therefore, the spring of friendship with the filth of concupiscence, and I beclouded its brightness with the hell of lustfulness." He struggled to contain the pleasures of the body. For a Christian at that time, it was clearly quite a task.

This approach continued in the Middle Ages and Renaissance. The work of early thinkers of the Catholic Church—including Clement of Alexandria, Tertullian, Basil, and Jerome—suggested that earthly love was a malady.

VA: What languages were spoken in the Garden of Eden?

IS: That question is at the core of a long debate.

VA: You wrote about it in your essay "The Verbal Quest."

IS: The difference between divine and human languages is dealt with in the Aggadah. The divine, it's believed, speaks solely in *lashon hakodesh*, a celestial tongue inaccessible to humans. The language of humankind is *lashon bnei adam*. Hebrew is the sacred language not because of its divine quality but because God chose it to communicate with his creation. Prior to the episode of the Tower of Babel, Adam and Eve's descendants used a single language. Was it Hebrew? If the answer is yes, it doesn't follow that Hebrew was the language spoken in the Garden of Eden. So what was it? Columbus, for one, thought that the Edenic languages were Chaldee and Hebrew.

VA: What did Columbus know about Eden?

IS: Stewart Lee Allen mentions in his book *In the Devil's Garden,* published in 2002, that Columbus was so sure of Eden's location that he brought two crew members fluent in these languages. When he bumped into South America, Columbus mistakenly thought that the Orinoco River in Venezuela was the gateway to Eden. And he brought back to Europe what the Hungarians call *paradicsom* (paradise), known in Latin as *poma amoris* (the love apple): the tomato, which Allen describes as "a slut-red fruit." In the sixteenth century Christians thought that tomatoes would make your teeth fall out; their smell would drive you insane. Those juices and seeds made it a naughty fruit, capable of inflaming passions in a way a brown potato couldn't be accused of doing. As Allen states, "The potato's chaste nature was further proven by its method of asexual reproduction: it has no seeds but instead creates offspring directly from its body."

VA: How is *sin* defined in the *OED*?

IS: The Oxford dons describe it as "an act which is regarded as a transgression of the divine law and an offense against God." The word might be related to the Latin *sont,* meaning guilty. There are also suspicions that in Old English, the word is connected to the original general *sense*, meaning "offense, wrong-doing, misdeed." In Spanish, the verb is *pecar* and the noun is *pecado*. In French, *pécher* and *péché*. In German, *sündigen* and *Sünde*.

Catholicism approaches it from that perspective. Sin, Saint Augustine argued in *Contra Faustum*, book 22, is "dictum vel factum vel concupitum contra legem æternam," a thought, word, or act done against "Eternal Law." Eternal Law for him is divine law as expressed through morality. According to the Decalogue and other codes established in the Bible—ethical, spiritual, intellectual, social, dietary—forbidden acts are sinful: incest, envy, ambitions, extramarital desire, and so on. To perform one of these acts is to sin; it's an attempt against the sanctity of God's creation.

In 1480, Hieronymus Bosch painted *The Table of the Cardinal Sins*, currently at the Museo de El Prado in Madrid. It was acquired by Philip II for his chambers in El Escorial. The design is circular against a square structure, and it contains several concentric circles, shaped in the form of a large eye. At the center of the eye is the image of Christ. The implication is that Jesus is at the center and oversees everything. Each of the cardinal sins is depicted, and outside the circle there are four images announcing the outcome of those sins: death, the Last Judgment, Hell, and glory.

VA : What does Judaism say about sin?

IS : The Tanakh is designed as a contract between the divine and the human. At the core of that contract is morality: to act ethically is to sanctify the divine. A person's life ought to be organized around the principles of morality. But there's no stress on the concept of sin. The Christian idea of "the fall" is alien to Jews. In Shakespeare's *Twelfth Night,* Feste claims, "Anything that's mended is but patched; virtue that transgresses is but patched with sin, and sin that amends is but patched with virtue" (1.5.47– 49). This is an utterly Christian view.

VA: I have an anecdote to tell you. Once, shortly after a horrendous Houston flood, I was teaching class. Neither my students nor I felt like working, so I decided instead to play a cultural list game. I started by asking about the wonders of the world (everyone knew there to be seven), then the number of continents (no one could agree on whether Europe and Asia should be counted separately, or whether India/Pakistan was a subcontinent). Next came sins and virtues. To my surprise, some of my Hispanic students told me that there were not just seven sins, but nine. The two additional ones are denying the Holy Ghost, *el Espíritu Santo,* and suicide.

IS: In his *Summa Theologica,* Thomas Aquinas lists seven cardinal sins: pride, avarice, gluttony, lust, sloth, envy, and ire (in Latin, *superbia, avaritia, gula, luxuria, acedia, invidia,* and *ira*). They were equated with seven demons. The same was established by theologians such as Saint Bonaventure, but the hierarchy has been endlessly debated and adapted. More recently, Konrad Lorenz, in his book *Die acht Todsünden der zivilisierten Menschheit,* translated into English in 1973 as

Civilized Man's Eight Deadly Sins, established that there are eight sins. Lorenz, a Viennese and also a Nobel Prize winner, was one of the founders of ethology, which studied inherited patterns of culture among animals and humans. Instead of using Catholic thought to elaborate his argument, he suggested eight challenges for society: overpopulation, detachment from the environment, self-competition, the paralyzation of human emotions, genetic decay, the loss of tradition, the emphasis on doctrine as a form of life, and the proliferation of nuclear weapons.

VA: Let's talk about gluttony. I want to begin with your story "The Disappearance." Its protagonist is a Belgian actor of mammoth proportions, whose appetite for food is unlimited. I understand that you wrote it at the request of the editor of an anthology about "the messy self."

IS: "The Disappearance" is based on a real-life incident in the Low Countries in 1988, in which a Shakespearean actor, Jules Croiset, a Jew, plotted his own kidnapping to call attention to the rise of neo-Nazism. After reading about it in the *New York Times,* I saved the news clipping for years, until the invitation to meditate on "the messy self" came about. The incident immediately came to mind. My central character's gluttony is based on an obsession with food I remember in a Holocaust survivor I met as a child in Mexico, a man who at first did menial jobs at a Yiddish day school and eventually became a famous theater director. To eat, for him, was to defy death.

VA : The story begins, "I wonder if stomach cancer is one of the prices one might pay for gluttony, for that is what killed Marteen Soëtendrop at the age of seventy-one."

IS : Soëtendrop's body is a reflection not only of his oversized personality but of the guilt he has accumulated since World War II. I was enchanted by the idea of an oversized actor who, in order to prove that a fascist group took advantage of him, needed to perform an acrobatic, self-flagellating act.

VA : Do you sometimes feel guilty when you eat?

IS : No. Personally, I'm not interested in meal sizes; instead, I'm interested in forbidden food.

VA : Such as?

IS : Maybe the ultimate guilt comes from eating foie gras, because the geese are force-fed to increase the size of their livers. But I believe that Stewart Lee Allen is right in that if guilt has flavor, it tastes like ortolans, the lemon-colored songbirds that first appeared in French chansons as symbols of innocence and the love of Jesus. The birds are about the size of a human toe and are illegal to hunt and to eat. They're captured alive and blinded or kept in a dark box for a month and fed millet, grapes, and figs. When they reach four times their original size, they are drowned in a snifter of Armagnac in order for their lungs to naturally baste their bodies with the spirit during roasting. Allen claims that François Mitterrand, in the last meal before his death, devoured them in the traditional manner, first covering his head with an embroidered cloth, then inserting the entire roasted bird into his mouth.

v A : To the believer, the divinity is the creator of all things. Why then should divinity prohibit certain kinds of food?

I S : Titus Lucretius Carus, who lived in 99–55 BCE, is credited for saying that "what is food to one is to others bitter poison."

v A : All great meals, it has been said, lead to discussions of either sex or death.

I S : Interestingly, Sigmund Freud has little to say about food. His writings are about psychological matters but hardly ever about the way the body and spirit interact. I find this omission astonishing, especially when one takes into consideration Freud's Jewish upbringing. Food was an essential component in his Viennese environment, but he is silent about it. In his case, the connection between food, sex, and death is incomplete. He delves amply into the latter two, but food is conspicuously absent.

v A : Is a love of food part of every religion?

I S : Not always. There are some branches that promulgate abstinence as a form of penitence, while others endorse a hermit existence based on only the very basic. And then there are mystical sects whose use of food—hallucinogens, for instance—becomes a tool to achieve alternate states of consciousness.

v A : Of the three Western religions, only Christianity does not establish strict dietary rules.

I S : For Christians the daily diet is a smaller part of the covenant. Fish replaces meat on Fridays. In Judaism and Islam, however, diet plays a predominant role. The issue of *kashrut* in Judaism is tied in with love, as specified by the Shehitah, the dietary laws that establish the way animal meat must be treated for it to be sanctified, the types of animals on earth and in water that may be consumed, how meat and dairy products must be kept separate, and so on. In Christianity, Christ's body becomes food. In Islam, the meat of a sanctified animal slaughtered in Allah's name is *Halal* (Qur'an 2:173 and 6:121). According to the Qur'an, slaughtering the animal in the name of someone else makes it sinful. But when an individual cannot control hunger, it is permissible to eat *Haram,* forbidden food (Qur'an 2:173, 6:145, 16:110, and 18:19). Christianity, in its anorexic approach to food, modeled itself as a reaction to the gastronomic and sexual decadence of the Roman Empire. In Arab civilization—as seen in pre-Islamic poetry, the Qur'an, the *Thousand and One Nights,* and the poetry of Ommar Khayam—food is a sign of enjoyment and refined manners.

In the Bible there are numerous food metaphors, some positive, others not. To describe the sins of Jerusalem, for instance, the Book of Ezekiel talks about turning the king of Babylon into a stew (24:3–136). The Song of Songs includes aphrodisiac and restorative ingredients (5:1–2). Then there's the infamous rape of Tamar by her brother Amnon, which brought about a civil war in ancient Israel. A sick Amnon asks his father to bring Tamar and make *levivot.* In Hebrew the word means cake, but its root is similar to *heart.*

The connection between feasts and abstinence is also part

of the modern nation-states. In regimes like Lenin's Russia, Mao's China, and Castro's Cuba, there was a celebration of hunger, not metaphorically but physically, as a political stand. That type of endurance, attached to a portrayal of excessive sexual activity as a capitalist indulgence, became a signature of those societies. Indeed, think of the archetypal Soviet woman of the 1940s: spayed, without sensuality. The body politic seemed to have required total sacrifice of any sense of individual glamour to an ideal of collectivism. After World War II, abortion was a frequent birth-control method. In Mao's time, there was even the concept of "eating bitterness" as a form of resistance against Western values. In Cuba the paradigm was a bit different. A woman's body was hers alone, and only she could choose how to make use of it. Sexual pleasure wasn't perceived as the domain of the bourgeoisie, as is clear in the novels by Pedro Juan Soto.

VA : At the same time, one often hears about "the hunger of the masses."

IS : Whenever the masses are in a state of unrest, the idea is to fill people's stomachs as soon as possible. In *The Underdogs,* a novel by Mariano Azuela on the Mexican Revolution of 1910, a meal becomes a palliative for anger. It makes me think of the famous quote misattributed to Marie Antoinette: "Qu'ils mangent de la brioche."

VA : In summary, what can we say about the requirements of taste?

IS : Love and beauty change from culture to culture and from one period to the next, as does taste. Our ideas, our looks, what we eat and drink, what we say and think—all are contingent on the factors that define us. Thus, it isn't absurd to state that beauty is always local, even in a global age like ours. We only love what we have been taught to.

V

A CATALOG OF PERVERSION

VA: You've touched on the idea of forbidden love . . .

IS: It's a variant of what Edgar Allan Poe called "the veneer of virtue." The etymology of the word *perversion,* as stated in the *OED,* placed it first and foremost in the realm of the physical: "the trace of a point whose direction of motion changes."

VA: Yet its modern use is about sexual depravity, isn't it?

IS: Yes, although *depravity* relates to moral corruption in general. Perversion refers to an aberrant, even abhorrent sexual practice that deviates from the normal standard. In other words, an *actus reus,* including such wrongful behavior as incest, sodomy, pedophilia, and zoophilia. Then there's chastity, which Aldous Huxley called the most unnatural of all sexual perversions. Perversion is defined by each culture in different ways.

VA: Still, there are always deviant patterns of sexual conduct.

I s : As long as there's a norm, there's a deviation. And deviations are always justifiable through love.

v a : Is prostitution part of the catalog of perversions?

I s : It's called the oldest profession in the world, as important as politics. It's legal in countless places. Prostitutes are frequently driven to their profession by necessity.

v a : Does a prostitute learn to love differently?

I s : I assume she must stop experiencing physical pleasure as a manifestation of affection. There are countless movies about the topic. Among the ones I remember best is Héctor Babenco's *Pixote,* about street orphans in São Paulo and Rio de Janeiro. There's a memorable scene in it in which the child protagonist cuddles with a prostitute. Then the camera focuses on the prostitute in the toilet. In the trash can rests a bloody fetus.

v a : Who's the first prostitute in history?

I s : There are numerous references to prostitution in the Bible. The cast includes prostitutes who perform sex for money and others who are forced into the profession after their husbands die. They sometimes perform benign acts. In the Book of Joshua, the prostitute Rahab helps Joshua's spies leave Jericho. And in the Book of Hosea, one of the twelve minor prophets, there are abundant references to harlots. The book chronicles the turbulent relationship between Hosea and his wife, Gomer, a prostitute he acquires for fifteen shekels and returns to the sanctity of the family home. The narrative establishes a relationship between physical prostitution and the prostitution that the people of Israel engage in when they embrace material fortune instead of the biblical Almighty.

Examples abound in ancient Rome, too. Brutus's mother, Servilia Caepionis, was Caesar's lover, and she ran successful houses of prostitution and, as a patrician, enjoyed considerable prestige. Upon Caesar's assassination by Brutus, and the final defeat of Antony, Octavian rose to power. He changed his name to Augustus and launched a moral crusade, promoting marriage, family, and childbirth while discouraging luxury, unrestrained sex, and adultery. Marriage laws, established to encourage the growth of the citizen population, brought back a more conservative moral foundation. Despite Augustus's good intentions, the revised marriage laws were largely unsuccessful.

A useful record for the Roman period might have been *Lives of the Prostitutes*, although the volume is lost. It was written by the first-century historian Suetonius, a friend of Pliny, who also wrote *De viris illustribus* (On Famous Literary Men), *De illustribus grammaticis* (Lives of the Grammarians), *De claris rhetoribus* (Lives of the Rhetoricians), and, most famously, *Lives of the Poets.* That Suetonius devoted equal energy to compiling a genealogy of whores offers a glimpse of their relevance in that period.

If one were to expand on Suetonius's list, the entries could include Mata Hari (she's credited as saying, "I am a woman who enjoys herself very much; sometimes I lose, sometimes I win"), Theodora, Christine Keeler, Sydney Biddle Barrows, the prostitutes of the Qing dynasty, both of Juan Domingo Perón's wives—Evita and Isabelita—and perhaps the Japanese geishas.

The number of literary works about prostitutes is endless. Shakespeare made several important references to prostitutes and their career. In *Much Ado about Nothing*, Beatrice responds to a betrothal offer from Don Pedro, the Prince of Aragon, who says to her, "Will you have me, lady?": "No, my lord, unless I might have another for working days: your grace is too costly to wear every day" (2.1.326–329). There's also Mistress Overdone in *Measure by Measure*. And some have read his sonnets to the Dark Lady as a rendezvous with a whore.

In Spanish-language letters alone there's a plethora of references to prostitution. Mario Vargas Llosa wrote about an escort service for the Peruvian army in his novel *Captain Pantoja and the Special Service*. Gabriel García Márquez's *Cándida Eréndira* is about a girl who, after accidentally burning her grandmother's property, is forced to repay her by becoming a prostitute. Isabel Allende has also made several contributions to the genre. And is Aldonza Lorenzo, the object of Don Quixote's passion, a prostitute, as she's portrayed at times? Not quite. She's "una moza labradora, de muy buen parecer, de quien él un tiempo anduvo enamorado, aunque, según se entiende, ella jamás lo supo ni le dio cata de ello," which J. M. Cohen's translates as "a very good-looking farm girl, whom he had taken with at one time, although she is supposed not to have known it or had proof of it." Cervantes wouldn't have described her as a *moza labradora* if in fact she was a *moza del partido,* as he described others. The one whose career is questionable is Aldonza Lorenzo's nemesis, Maritornes, the ugly and loose servant girl.

VA : In Spanish there's the term *meretriz.*

IS : It refers to someone who uses her sexual tools to achieve power. Thus, it's connected with merit. In English, though, the implication is different: *meretricious,* meaning tasteless, showy, based on pretense.

VA : The flip side of the coin is the art of soliciting sex.

IS : Who is it that said that if the powerful use their influence to solicit sex, then often the weak use sex to solicit influence?

VA : The solicitation, when coming from the mighty, results in scandal.

IS : Love and scandal. Have we finally reached the core of our discussion?

VA : Bill Clinton got caught in the White House.

IS : It wasn't a solicitation, though. There was no monetary transaction. Instead, it was consensual sex. The nature of the relationship was explosive, however. He was the president of the United States, a married man with a daughter in college, and an inexperienced intern, Monica Lewinsky, who by the way was no innocent maiden. This sort of encounter is typical almost everywhere in the world, from France to Mexico. Yet in the United States, where puritanism still runs rampant, it became news, even though John F. Kennedy also engaged in similar extramarital affairs.

VA : Is this type of affair a perversity?

IS : No, it's human nature.

VA : How does it fit into the architectural design you've proposed?

IS : The locus of illicit love is the basement, which is a metaphor for any secluded—that is, forbidden—love. The term *illicit* is somewhat elastic, taken to mean not only illegal but also close, furtive, surreptitious, and clandestine. The Hispanic poet Delmira Agustini's strange affair with her own husband, which I talked about before, is an example. In the end, he fired two bullets at her head and then killed himself. Or think of Aleksandr Pushkin's *Secret Journal.* Fatally wounded in a duel with his brother-in-law and rival in 1837, Pushkin left behind a secret, ciphered diary and instructed that it not be published until one hundred years after his death. Some people describe it as a hoax. It consists of explicit confessions about the intimate relationships Pushkin had with his wife, her two sisters, and other women, which might have brought him to his tragic end. One should never underestimate the twists and turns of the human heart.

VA : Are you talking about imagined love, the kind that appears only in our most intimate thoughts?

IS : That love is essential to me. To what extent is the imagined love, as you call it, an actual love? We all have secrets. Indeed, our psychological life is defined by the currents of consciousness that only we know about. But those secret thoughts are never abstract. Nor are they innocent. They infringe on everything we do. Our imagination is the freest of all our capacities, but it is also the most dangerous. Can we control it? It's a well-known fact that any love affair involves not two but four lovers: two actual and two imagined. The difference between my real lover and the lover I imagine is as important as the difference between me and the person she imagines me to be.

I'm fascinated with dreams. I keep a record of the dreams I've had and, to the extent possible, I incorporate those dreams (or the anecdotes I turn them into) into everything I do: stories, essays, newspaper columns, my teaching, lectures, breakfast and dinner conversations. I don't care about Freud's manual of interpretation. In other words, I don't care about what the dreams mean. Instead, I'm interested in them as a form of storytelling, one in which the teller and the listener are one and the same. How are dreams narrated? Where do they start and finish? How do they deliver the plot? How do they construct atmosphere? What kind of aftertaste do they leave us with?

One day I'd like to write a short history of dreams. Kafka experienced sinister dreams, which he recounted in his diaries about lost loves, whereas for Marcel Proust in *Remembrance of Things Past,* dreams are ruminations on the implacability of the waking world. Wouldn't it be marvelous to retrace the history of humankind not through its actions but through its dreams? The German critic Walter Benjamin was an assiduous chronicler of his dreams. So were the British art critic John Ruskin and the poet Stephen Spender, as well as André Breton, Ovid, Saint Augustine, Flaubert, Thomas de Quincy, Kafka, Marcel Proust, Joseph Conrad, and Borges. There are plenty of significant love dreams that we should pay attention to. "I dreamt I dwelt in marble halls, / And each damp thing that creeps and crawls / Went wobble-wobble on the walls"— do Lewis Carroll's lines from "The Palace of Humbug" refer to love and sex? We ought to understand, not in Freudian terms but in more creative ones, the way our dreams infringe upon us, defining who we are and how we act.

Among my favorite love dreams is one by Samuel Taylor Coleridge. The legend that surrounds it—much repeated, much revised—is symptomatic of the hallucinatory quality of the dream itself. Sometime in the autumn of 1797, after an exhausting day, Coleridge smoked opium, a legal substance at the time and one regularly used for medical reasons and also to elevate one's level of awareness. In a farmhouse near Exmoor, he had a dream—a divine revelation?—in which a poem came to him. It would eventually be called "Kubla Khan." Upon waking, he wrote fifty-four lines. Then someone from the nearby town, whom he described as "the person from Porlock," knocked at the door. He went to the door, and when he returned to his desk to continue the composition, the inspiration was gone. Coleridge's poem is subtitled "A Vision in a Dream: A Fragment." I find it inexhaustible:

In Xanadu did Kubla Khan
A stately pleasure dome decree:
Where Alph, the sacred river, ran
Through caverns measureless to man

Down to a sunless sea.
So twice five miles of fertile ground
With walls and towers were girdled round:
And there were gardens bright with sinuous rills,
Where blossomed many an incense-bearing tree;
And here were forests ancient as the hills,
Enfolding sunny spots of greenery.

But oh! that deep romantic chasm which slanted
Down the green hill athwart a cedarn cover!
A savage place! as holy and enchanted
As e'er beneath a waning moon was haunted
By woman wailing for her demon lover!
And from this chasm, with ceaseless turmoil seething,
As if this earth in fast thick pants were breathing,
A mighty fountain momently was forced:
Amid whose swift half-intermitted burst
Huge fragments vaulted like rebounding hail,
Or chaffy grain beneath the thresher's flail:
And 'mid these dancing rocks at once and ever
It flung up momently the sacred river.
Five miles meandering with a mazy motion
Through wood and dale the sacred river ran,
Then reached the caverns measureless to man,
And sank in tumult to a lifeless ocean:
And 'mid this tumult Kubla heard from far
Ancestral voices prophesying war!

The shadow of the dome of pleasure
Floated midway on the waves;
Where was heard the mingled measure
From the fountain and the caves.
It was a miracle of rare device,
A sunny pleasure dome with caves of ice!

A damsel with a dulcimer
In a vision once I saw:
It was an Abyssinian maid,
And on her dulcimer she played,
Singing of Mount Abora.
Could I revive within me
Her symphony and song,
To such a deep delight 'twould win me,
That with music loud and long,
I would build that dome in air,
That sunny dome! those caves of ice!
And all who heard should see them there,
And all should cry, Beware! Beware!
His flashing eyes, his floating hair!
Weave a circle round him thrice,
And close your eyes with holy dread,
For he on honey-dew hath fed,
And drunk the milk of Paradise.

Coleridge dwells on love as an exotic emotion. The pleasure-
dome in Xanadu was the summer retreat created in what is

today Mongolia, in China, by Kublai Khan, the thirteenth-century Mongol monarch of the Yuan Dynasty, grandson of Genghis Khan. Coleridge imagines it as three concentric circles, an image that returns again toward the end of the poem when the poet speaks of himself: "weave a circle round him thrice." In other words, there is symmetry between outer and inner worlds. At the heart of the pleasure-dome is the nonexistent, primordial Alph River, whose name invokes the first letter of the Hebrew and Greek alphabets. An underground portion of the river is made of icy caverns "measureless to man" that result in a central fountain erupting in a "half-intermitted burst" of "huge fragments vaulted like rebounding hail." Then there's the Abyssinian girl. For us the word *Abyssinian* means Ethiopian. Coleridge visualized a maiden that was as exotic—and un-British—as possible. Not surprisingly, Edward Said placed "Kubla Khan" in the history of European Orientalism. In his dream, the poet hopes to embrace the girl playing the dulcimer. Is this a portrait of sexual fantasy?

VA : Who was the person from Porlock?

IS : The equivalent of the UPS guy today. Coleridge wrote (in third person) in a piece that accompanied the poem: "On awakening he appeared to himself to have a distinct recollection of the whole, and taking his pen, ink, and paper, instantly and eagerly wrote down the lines that are here preserved. At this moment he was unfortunately called out by a person on business from Porlock, and detained by him above an hour, and on his return to his room, found, to his no small surprise and mortification, that though he still retained some vague and dim recollection of the general purport of the vision, yet, with the exception of some eight or ten scattered lines and images, all the rest had passed away like the images on the surface of a stream into which a stone has been cast, but, alas! without the after restoration of the latter!'"

Ay, the ephemerality of dreams! Coincidentally, Kublai Khan is said to have envisioned the summer retreat of Xanadu in a dream.

VA: You wondered whether Coleridge's dream should be understood as revelation.

IS: For the Romantics, poetic inspiration and prophetic revelation were almost identical—the poet was seen as a sort of celestial mouthpiece. The composition of "Kubla Khan," shaped by inspiration, reminds me of Muhammad receiving each verse of the Qur'an from Allah in the first part of the seventh century, and in turn delivering them to the people of Mecca.

VA: Returning to your architectural metaphor, are dreams another type of basement?

IS: They represent hidden, forbidden, or secluded desires. Is there someone who doesn't dream of a private Xanadu?

VA: What function do you ascribe to dreams in love?

IS: Even when we're alone, dreams keep us company. They allow us to imagine a thousand different lovers, to engage in lovemaking in unforeseen ways.

A form of dreaming is our ongoing need to wish. In love, as

in life, we're always wishing for something. There's a persistent rumor about William Blake's wish to engage in polygamy even though he and his wife, Kate, apparently lived happily together. Every so often he would casually mention the possibility of getting a second wife, and Kate's reaction invariably involved tears. Indeed, William Butler Yeats wrote, confirming the rumor, "It is said that Blake wished to add a concubine to his establishment in the Old Testament manner, but gave up the project because it made Mrs. Blake cry." Whatever the truth, the anecdote is about marital angst and about Blake's wishes, which, in and of themselves, constitute an alternative form of life.

Conceived as a single, uninterrupted narrative, dreams are proof that beyond what our senses register, beyond what we call reality, there's a parallel universe, a universe ruled by a different logic, where it rains but one doesn't get wet, where one might at one moment be a knife and at the next an elephant. Yes, dreams are an alternative geography, with its own aesthetic of beauty and its own concept of love, a geography where death isn't the end. Through love, art, and philosophy, we attempt an approximation of that geography. Years ago I happened to discover a delicious book by Alberto Manguel, *The Dictionary of Imaginary Places,* which is a register of fictional sites, from Thomas Moore's Utopia to Umberto Eco's monastery in *The Name of the Rose.* In *Undr,* Jorge Luis Borges frees signs from their signifiers and makes them capable of triggering revelations that are almost magical. The novel is set in Urnland, an imaginary place described by Adam of Bremen in the eleventh century. Its inhabitants, the Urns, live in a few villages of wood and mud in the lowlands of the Vistula. The whole of Urn literature, the whole of their language, consists of one word, *undr,* which means "wonder." In that word any and all listeners will recognize the things they have seen, the people they have known, their loves, their desires, their secrets. And speaking of imaginary places, Frigyes Karinthy's *Capillaria,* about a submarine realm of the same name where men are unknown, has Oihas, female creatures who live entirely for pleasure. The Oihas—a word that can be translated as either "human being" or "perfection of nature"—are descended from the first Oiha, a self-impregnating creature. The original Oiha eliminated from her body the uncomfortable and ugly organ that performed the impregnation within her. Ever since, the organ has continued to exist as an external parasite, some ten inches long with a cylindrical body, a human face, and a bald head. The Oihas eat these parasites, called bullpops, which allows them to reproduce. When they give birth to other Oihas, hundreds of bullpops emerge from the womb and float around until they are eaten. In these imaginary places love occurs in ways unknown to us, yet it is still love.

VA : Dreams also create monsters, creatures with a strange appearance.

IS : Strange and frightening. In dreams it is possible to love and be frightened by a monster. No thorough discussion of love should take place without an examination of monstrosity. Samuel Johnson, in *A Dictionary of the English Language,* de-

fined *monster* as "something out of the common order of nature." The description is fitting, for love pushes us to reach the
edges of nature. Greek mythology is filled with examples of
pairings between animals and humans, and these are usually
violent: a bull abducts Europa, an eagle rapes Ganymede. But
there's the interesting case of Leda receiving the Jovian swan,
which, in my view, is far removed from bestiality. The golem
devised by the Maharal of Prague also comes to mind. And in
The Carnal Prayer Mat, written in seventeenth-century China,
the protagonist has his penis replaced by that of a dog, which
makes me think of the Sileni and Satyrs, those mostly benign,
good-natured, and rather boisterous creatures of the forest
who were the retinue of Dionysos, the god of wine. Notice
that Dr. Johnson's definition doesn't portray monsters as en-
gines of terror. It is suitable to conceive of extraordinary creatures as manifestations of our deepest fears but also as emblems of innate affection. I once dreamed of a monster made
of keys and staples. In its mouth it had a tongue made of ice.
Its fingers appeared to be white sausages; they were thin and
long. And it had wings that smelled liked burnt rubber. But
somehow I wasn't afraid. Instead, I felt tenderness.

v a : Monsters are also symbols.

i s : They might symbolize the thirst for knowledge, the embrace
of purity, and the fear of amoral encounters. And honor, of
course.

v a : Another item in the catalog of perversion is pedophilia.

i s : Pedophilia, and pederasty, too. They are sometimes taken to be the same thing, but most often the first is considered to be sex with children and the second anal sex performed by an adult male on a male child. Such acts seem not to have been infrequent in antiquity. It's shocking to us to read of the casual way in which Greek adults engaged in encounters with the young. While Western civilization forbids them, these acts have always been approached rather licentiously in some cultures. Examples include Martial's pederastic themes of the first century as well as the natural tone Lawrence Durrell uses to describe pedophilia in Levant after World War II in his novel *Justine,* an installment of his tetralogy on Alexandria first published in 1957. Acts of pedophilia occur in *Les Chançons de Bilitis* (1894) and *Aphrodite* (1896) by Pierre Louÿs, another "adopted" Alexandrian. Child sexuality is alive and well in the United States and Europe as well, at least judging by the Internet. It is taboo because in regard to carnal encounters, Western civilization places the emphasis on consent. Sex for us is a matter of responsibility. Responsibility is knowledge.

The stories of catamites, male children kept by pederasts, ranging from Ganymede to Saint Pelagius to the desire of Mehmet the Conqueror for Jacob Notaras, are illustrative of love and honor. When Lukas Notaras refuses to hand over his handsome youngest son, Jacob, to Mehmet, he does so out of a belief that the sultan will use the boy for deviant sexual pleasures that fit in with the Christian conception of the Turks as dogs incapable of nobler feelings common to civilized men.

The Turks, however, when informed of Notaras's refusal, speak of the Christians as incapable of understanding either mundane or metaphoric love.

V A : Homosexuality is still perceived as depraved by conservatives.

I S : Unfortunately. They fail to recognize its beauty.

V A : Did the high cultures of Greco-Roman antiquity take an indulgent view of it?

I S : Historian Paul Veyne said that in antiquity love of men for boys and women was considered one and the same. Foucault agreed. He believed that the Greeks didn't see love for one's own sex and love for the other sex as opposites. There is room for disagreement, but it's certainly possible that in Greco-Latin society there was no distinction between homosexuality and heterosexuality. Some of Martial's epigrams and Catullus's poems are about homosexuality, and Sappho wrote about lesbian love in her lyrics, which were meant to be sung or recited in public.

V A : How should one explain, then, the continued current attitudes condemning homosexuality?

I S : The power of religion is to blame. Christianity, Judaism, and Islam condemn it. They define it as unnatural.

V A : Meaning outside nature?

I S : Meaning unacceptable within the parameters of nature. Religion argues that animals don't engage in homosexual encounters, even though there are countless examples among animals of homosexual acts.

Still, heterosexual sex is a cornerstone of monotheistic religions. They support a biological—that is, reproductive—understanding of intercourse. The mandate to procreate, to multiply, is described as holy. The Catholic Church in particular also endorses chastity. There are abundant condemning examples of homosexual love in the Bible. Thus, conservative commentators use the Old Testament as proof of the unholiness of same-sex relations. In fact, our acceptance of homosexuality is an embrace of Athens and a rejection of Jerusalem.

v a : What are some instances in the Bible?

i s : Take Leviticus 18:22: "You shall not lie with a male as with a woman; it is an abomination." The passage equates homosexuality with bestiality. There are also references in Judges and Samuel 1 and 2. There are scholars who interpret the relationship in the Book of Ruth 1:14–18 between Naomi and Ruth as lesbian. Then there's the episode of Genesis 19, about Sodom and Gomorra, which, according to the biblical narrative, were immoral cities. To this day the word *sodomize* means to perform an array of homosexual—mostly male—acts. The *OED* repeats this view, defining *sodomy* as "an unnatural form of sexual intercourse, especially that of one male with another." There are also references in the New Testament, especially in the Gospel of Matthew.

v a : Have you ever loved another man?

i s : Yes, of course.

v a : Is masturbation also a perversity? Or is it a variety of self-love?

I S : The word *masturbation,* according to the *Encyclopedia Bri-*
tannica, refers to the "erotic stimulation of one's own genital
organs, usually to achieve orgasm" and "is common in infants
and adolescents, and is indulged in by many adults as well."
The history of onanism, as masturbation is also known, is rife
with misunderstandings. Studies done by Alfred Kinsey in
the 1950s indicated that some 90 percent of males and approximately 60 to 80 percent of females in the United States
masturbated at one time or another. Yet in the major Western
religions there's a prohibition against it: one's own body
shouldn't be the object of self-induced pleasure. There are
passing mentions of masturbation in the Bible, including
Leviticus 15:16–18, 15:32–33, and 22:4, and Deuteronomy
23:10–11. None of these passages refer to the emission of
semen as a sin, however. Such an emission has fewer consequences than a woman's menstruation. In Genesis 38:8–10, in
a genealogy of Judah and his daughter-in-law Tamar, the character Onan—from whom we get the word *onanism*—becomes
an emblem of self-provoked pleasure, if for the wrong reasons.
The passage in the King James Version describes Judah's son
Er, who is married to Tamar, as "a wicked man," a biblical reference to having a questionable character, and the divine kills
him. Judah then instructs his son Onan: "Go in unto thy
brother's wife, and marry her, and raise up seed to thy brother."
The levirate (in Spanish, *levirato;* in Hebrew, *ibum*) was the
standard approach at the time: when a husband died, his
widow would be married to his brother. But Onan believes at

this point that Tamar is already pregnant with Er's semen. The translation states, "And Onan knew that the seed should not be his; and it came to pass, when he went in unto his brother's wife, that he spilled *it* on the ground, lest that he should give seed to his brother. And the thing which he did displeased the Lord: wherefore he slew him also." In the original the semen is referred to tangentially as *zera,* which also has other meanings, including seed and descendants. Notice the word that the translators use: it. Perhaps the biblical story isn't about masturbation. After all, Onan doesn't generate his own pleasure. Instead, his tale is about coitus interruptus.

Spilling of semen without a deliberate intention to procreate is an offense in Judaism, especially in the Talmud. Coitus interruptus, nonvaginal sex, anal intercourse . . . in short, any form of sexual encounter not leading to pregnancy is considered sinful. The ideal of sexual purity was connected with marriage. That purity, however, ought to be taken with caution. Some, like Huguccio of Pisa in the thirteenth century, decreed that pleasure during intercourse by the married couple was a sin, even when the objective was to bear children. Abstention was the desired choice, and it was encouraged during numerous dates in the calendar, including Holy Communion, Lent, and other Christian holidays, not to mention during menstruation and while the mother was lactating. Extramarital sex was, of course, anathema. Witches were often considered to be not only elicitors but evil-worshipping promoters of such illicit encounters. In a famous manual of sexology called

Malleus Maleficarum, which was used as a tool for witch hunting, the definition of *carum* is the sexual act that "caused the corruption of our first parents, and, by its contagion, brought the inheritance of original sin upon the whole human race."

VA : How do other religions view masturbation?

IS : In Catholicism, at least since Saint Augustine, it's an affront to chastity. Protestantism also condemns it.

VA : How about Islam?

IS : Islam suggests that masturbation—*istimna* in Arabic—is allowed only to prevent adultery.

VA : Yet secular society is lenient toward masturbation.

IS : Kant believed masturbation went against natural law. But after the Enlightenment, views on sexual self-pleasure became varied. In the film *Annie Hall,* Woody Allen states, "Don't knock masturbation. It's sex with someone I love." Foucault was insightful on the concept of physical pleasure in Western civilization. He studied the pleasure attained in specific coordinates of time and space, and based on accepted institutions, such as marriage, prostitution, and so on. Indeed, in medieval times continuous engagement in masturbatory pleasure gave place to illnesses such as tuberculosis, gangrene, and apoplexy. It was thought that it might even bring about death. Diogenes the Cynic, according to Galen, masturbated in order to get rid of sexual desire. "If only I could remedy hunger by rubbing my hand on my belly!" Galen stated.

VA : Masturbation as part of a sexual encounter isn't forbidden.

IS : In fact, the caressing and rubbing of different sexual organs is often an essential part of the ritual (although outside ejaculation might still be condemned). Masturbation as part of intercourse is mentioned in the *Kama Sutra*. The actual coupling serves as the climax. (What can and cannot be done, however, depends on one's position in society. The *auparishkata,* or mouth union, for instance, isn't allowed among literate Brahmins, public servants devoted to state affairs, or men with a good reputation to protect.) Emanuel Swedenborg, in his *Journal of Dreams,* written between 1744 and 1745, described the difficult discipline required to control and manipulate the sexual energies. Despite the intensely erotic character of the images he visualized (while meditating upon the male and female Hebrew letters and Sephiroth), he could not dissipate his sexual energies in masturbation, nocturnal emission, or premature ejaculation.

VA : Masturbation is associated with the night.

IS : More than with the night, it is associated with a secret, private, self-provoked emission, although not always as a result of manipulation. The concept of a "wet dream," for instance, is connected with masturbation. It is also an extension of the disquisition on dreams I engaged in earlier. A dream with sexual elements might result in ejaculation. Yet the Bible does talk about "nocturnal emissions." *Deuteronomy* 23:9–11 argues for separating those in the community undergoing such experiences: "When the host goeth forth against thine enemies, then keep thee from every wicked thing. If there be among you any man, that is not clean by reason of uncleanness that chanceth him by night, then shall he go abroad out of the camp, he shall not come within the camp. But it shall be, when evening cometh on, he shall wash himself with water: and when the sun is down, he shall come into the camp again." In the English Standard Version, "reason of uncleanness that chanceth him by night" is called "nocturnal emission."

V A : There are a considerable number of slang terms to describe masturbation.

I S : Ay, ay, ay—in English, there's "flying solo" and "spanking the monkey." In Mexican Spanish, *hacerse la chaqueta* and *divertirse con el enano.* In France one might say *se taper la colonne* and in Canada *se passer un poignet.* In German, *sich einen runterholen, sich einen von der palme wedeln,* and *sich selbst befriedigen.* In Portuguese, *punhetar, sair na mão,* and *bater punheta.* Each language has its own possibilities.

V A : Have you heard of the masturbate-a-thon?

I S : No.

V A : It's a public event devoted to safe sex.

I S : An absurd example of the modern obsession with making sexuality a spectacle. By the way, there are numerous references to masturbation in literature, music, art, movies, and TV, from ancient Indian and Japanese paintings, Renaissance imagery, and the work of Gustav Klimt to Mark Twain, James Joyce, Allen Ginsberg (who supposedly got his inspiration for "Howl" while masturbating with a broom), John Lennon, and Bruce Springsteen. And it's a favorite topic in comedy, as you might imagine—there's the popular Seinfeld episode about being "master of your domain."

VA : I can't think of the Spanish word for foreplay. Is it that Latin lovers don't take the time or is it that when they engage in sex, they don't play?

IS : There are only awkward statements such as *caricias eróticas,* a kind of erotic caress. The French language doesn't have an equivalent either; the closest it comes is *excitacion préliminaire.* In Portuguese it's *as preliminares;* in Italian, *i preludi.* German speakers seem to have an equivalent: *Vorspiel.* In Hebrew it's *misjak makdim.*

VA : Moving to another topic, let's talk about harm in love.

IS : In *On Liberty,* John Stuart Mill suggests that the purpose of law ought to be to stop people from harming others. It's the concept of negative liberty, which Isaiah Berlin also explored. If lovers want to do something that results in a self-inflicted wound, the law shouldn't intercede, because they are sovereigns of their own domain. Mill argues, "The sole end for which mankind is warranted, individually or collectively, in interfering with the liberty of action of any of their number, is self-protection. [And t]he only purpose for which power can be rightfully exercised over any member of a civilised community, against his will, is to prevent harm to others. His own good, either physical or moral, is not sufficient warrant. He cannot rightfully be compelled to do or forbear because it will be better for him to do so, because it will make him happier, because, in the opinion of others, to do so would be wise, or even right. . . . Over himself, over his own body and mind, the individual is sovereign." The argument isn't about individualism but about morality. A set of standards applies not to limit self-wounds but to establish the parameters of social behavior.

VA: I read a case not long ago of an adult and a fourteen-year-old from Nebraska who fell in love. In order to live together, they crossed the state line into Kansas, where they weren't prosecuted.

IS: Standards vary. And then there's art, using pedophilia to test those standards. The case of Nabokov's *Lolita* is intriguing. No mainstream publisher in New York wanted to touch a manuscript about the obsession of Humbert Humbert with a pubescent girl. It was finally released in Paris by Olympia Press, a publisher of erotica, in 1955 and quickly became a cause célèbre. It was initially banned in the United States, but today it's easily available. Does that mean we've become more accepting?

VA: Acceptance may be due to the United States becoming more globalized. After all, where you and I come from, rural brides are often of an age that in the United States would be below the age of consent. But in Mexico—and elsewhere—consensual sex at an early age is far from being considered statutory rape. What about another facet of forbidden love—incest?

IS: Desiring one's parent, sibling, or child is taboo for us. Yet history is replete with examples—think of the royal dynasties alone. Likewise, literature, mythology, art, and folklore abound in scenes of incest, from the Bible to the Icelandic sagas, from *Oedipus Rex* to Shakespeare, from *One Hundred Years of Solitude* to *Star Wars*. The Old Testament story of Lot and his daughters is a classic tale of incest. There's also the famous passage in *Hamlet* in which Gertrude says, "Come higher, my dear Hamlet, sit by me." Hamlet responds, "No, good mother. Here's metal more attractive" (3.2.108–109). It seems that although love clashes with the prohibition against desiring a person of one's own immediate circle, the recurrence of such encounters is ongoing. In endogamic cultures, incest was a fixture of life. But genetics and morality shaped the exogamic parameters of Western civilization. Inbreeding among members of the same chromosome group leads to an increase in homozygosis.

VA : And, thus, the threat of birth defects. On the topics of conjugal relations, reproduction, and the interior life of the family, I would like to bring John Boswell into the conversation. Boswell, known primarily for his pioneering work in queer studies, argued in *The Kindness of Strangers: The Abandonment of Children in Western Europe from Late Antiquity to the Renaissance* (1989) that family connections "are among the most reclusive and private aspects of human existence, jealously guarded from public view in most cultures, and less likely than almost any other interpersonal activity to leave written records." He further argued that they are unusually resistant to modern investigative techniques.

IS : Boswell was an advocacy scholar. He based this particular thesis on David Herlihy's studies brought to light in *Medieval Children,* published in 1978. Herlihy said that "of all social groups which formed the societies of the past, children, seldom seen and rarely heard in the documents, remain for historians the most elusive, the most obscure."

v a : Relying on historical records for researching the inner life of the family is difficult enough, but relying on literature—imaginative literature in particular—to understand earlier societies is dangerous.

i s : True—literature isn't testimony. The line between truth and deception is too thin.

v a : I'm thinking specifically of Boswell's "quicksand problem."

i s : Yes, an ingenious if almost treacherous argument by Boswell. In *The Kindness of Strangers* he claims that we are so familiar with the perils of quicksand that not only do we all know that the more you move the quicker you sink, but we also have detailed instructions stored in our brains that would allow us to rescue someone trapped in such a pit. Because of the ubiquitous presence of quicksand in literature and movies—from Westerns to David Lean's *Lawrence of Arabia* to Mel Brooks's *Blazing Saddles*—it would seem to constitute a real peril to anyone who dares to go out for a walk. In reality, however, it's possible that no real person has ever died in quicksand or even needed to be rescued from it. As Boswell states, "I have never met a person with a friend, relative or casual acquaintance who has been incommoded in any way by quicksand, despite its pivotal role in the lives of many citizens of fiction." In other words, quicksand may be nothing more than a convenient plot device to get rid of good characters with pathos or bad ones with justice, or simply to create tension.

The fact that we don't find many references to, say, abortion in earlier literature may be because abortion is of little use to an author, who would, after all, be killing off a potential protagonist. But the lack of references does not mean that the practice didn't take place. Boswell also mentions the case of adultery. Adultery is an extremely convenient plot device that offers excuses for murders, jealousies, false suspicions, and, as Boswell puts it, "new groupings of major characters." It is so prevalent in literature that one might suspect that it was invented for fiction, regardless of whether it occurred in real life. We could even venture a guess and say that most adults would assume that adultery is more common in fiction than in real life. In fact, the case is nearly the reverse. Boswell says that "most fictional occurrences of adultery are limited to key characters in the story; the rest of the population is presumed—by implicit contrast if not explicit description—to be faithfully married." In real life, adultery is not limited to leading characters, and it isn't necessarily a major traumatic event as it is portrayed in fiction. Furthermore, it can hardly be considered uncommon. Boswell provides evidence—based on Kinsey's controversial studies—that shows that even in the 1940s, long before the sexual revolution, about half of all married men in the United States had intercourse with women other than their wives. Incest is another convenient plot device for authors. It is used all the time in literature.

VA : So, is incest a quicksand problem?

IS : While it might not have been as prevalent a feature of earlier societies as literature suggests, it's clear from the scholarship by Boswell and others that incest, like the abandonment of children, was part of the landscape. There is enough evidence to show that it was practiced then and is with us today.

VA: Psychoanalysis dwells on the topic.

IS: Incessantly. The Oedipus complex, and to a lesser extent the Electra complex, are at the core of Freud's theory of sexuality and guilt.

VA: Guilt being another important facet of forbidden love.

IS: In the story "The Grand Inquisitor," included in Dostoyevsky's *The Brothers Karamazov,* the inquisitor says, "There is no such thing as a plea of innocence in my court. A plea of innocence is guilty of wasting my time." The statement applies to sex in general. Of course, taboos such as incest amplify the feeling of being remorsefully aware of committing a forbidden act.

VA: What about lovesickness?

IS: In Renaissance Europe, a malady of widespread proportions was recognized: lovesickness. It was believed that an excess of black bile—a kind of sluggish humor—took over the brain. When someone fell in love but the feeling was not reciprocated, this substance would bring forth physical and mental deterioration. It was also believed that lovesickness came about when a person went without sex for an extended period of time. In the case of men, physicians would often recommend as a cure a visit to the brothel. It wasn't important who the person had intercourse with as long as the toxins were ejected from the body. Another medical approach was blood-letting. The rationale was that the buildup of black bile needed to be balanced out by reducing another of the humors. Some years ago I read a thought-provoking book, *The Wages of Sin,* by Peter Lewis Allen, about the cultural ramifications of lovesickness. The topic is also explored in Robert Graves's "Symptoms of Love":

Love is a universal migraine,
A bright stain on the vision
Blotting out reason.

Symptoms of true love
Are leanness, jealousy,
Laggard dawns;

Are omens and nightmares—
Listening for a knock,
Waiting for a sign:

For a touch of her fingers
In a darkened room,
For a searching look.

Take courage, lover!
Can you endure such grief
At any hand but hers?

Love as illness, love as nightmare, love as curse . . . yet, also, love as a form of courage. But what is love? Neither Shakespeare nor Graves comes close to defining it, but it isn't their limitation. Love's boundaries are deliberately unspecified. Ask a dozen people what love is, and you're likely to get a dozen different definitions.

VA: One of the symptoms Graves talks about is jealousy.

IS: The suspicion of being replaced by a rival. At some point we all feel the same type of apprehension: the lover is ours alone and not to be shared. Jealousy is about envy and resentment, protectiveness and distrust. It's a natural component of love. But an excess of it becomes maddening. The lover no longer is able to believe in the partner. Everything poses a threat.

Love and jealousy, love and madness: *l'amour fou.* In Plato's *Phaedrus,* love is presented as "divine madness." There are countless examples of mad love in history. Among the most famous I know is the story of Juana of Castile, better known as Juana la Loca, the unstable Spanish queen at the dawn of the sixteenth century. She was part of a distinguished lineage, being the second daughter of Ferdinand of Aragon and Isabelle of Castile, who supported all four of Columbus's voyages and who orchestrated the so-called Reconquista, unifying Spain under Catholicism. Her sister was Catherine of Aragon, first wife of Henry VIII. Juana was the wife of Philip the Handsome, and the mother of Charles V, the ruler of a kingdom "en el que nunca se pone el sol" (in which the sun does not set).

Jealousy was the source of Juana's *locura,* her madness. Philip was a philanderer. Their relationship, however, was a roller coaster from the outset. Juana was betrothed to Philip as a strategy to expand the Spanish Empire. The moment they met it was love at first sight. They made love madly and were officially married the following day. Later, Juana became suspicious, then resentful, of his sexual escapades. When Philip died of typhoid fever in 1506, Juana's stability quickly deteriorated. She kept his coffin at her side and opened it to kiss his feet. She also refused to bathe. Her father, ambitious as he was, eventually imprisoned her for years in a castle in Tordesillas, in the province of Valladolid, keeping her away from the power she rightfully inherited. She died in 1555, at the age of seventy-six.

There's a painting at the Casón del Buen Retiro by Francisco Pradilla Ortiz, a prolific nineteenth-century realist artist famous for depicting historical scenes, portraying Juana la Loca as a distressed widow, dressed in black, standing at the side of her late husband's coffin. The landscape is ominous. A procession of women accompanies Juana in her grief. Her facial expression is ghastly.

VA: I'm interested in lovesickness. But let's start with the meaning of the word *humor.*

IS: Today it's used to describe the capacity to laugh. It also refers to a person's good nature. But in the twelfth century it referred to something different: four mysterious substances found in the body and capable of affecting every dimension of life.

VA : One of these humors, black bile, triggered melancholy.

IS : From the Greek *melan-*, black, plus *chole,* bile, melancholy is a popular topic in art and literature. Romantic literature in particular is replete with characters suffering from this malady. Jan Havicksz Steen's painting *The Lovesick Maiden* comments sarcastically on doctors attempting to cure lovesickness. A doctor attempts to diagnose a young lady, but the Dutch painter announces the real reason for her sickness: there is an image of Cupid on top of the door. Might she be longing for her lover? Why is the bed unmade? To me the painting is about the impact of absence on love. Or maybe about the illness that results from a double loyalty. There's also a story by Uruguayan writer Horacio Quiroga—whom Borges once said rewrote poorly the stories Edgar Allan Poe had already written well—called "El almohadón de plumas" (The Feather Pillow), about a lovesick bride forced to stay in bed. As days and nights go by, she loses not only weight but her joie de vivre, as if it were being sucked up by a mysterious monster. Eventually, she dies. Soon after her death, they discover that under her feather pillow was a leach.

The modern word for lovesickness is *depression.* The sense that love is connected to sadness is pervasive. Think of Neruda's famous line: "Puedo escribir los versos más tristes esta noche," translated by W. S. Merwin as "Tonight I can write the saddest lines." In Gabriel García Márquez's *Love in the Time of Cholera,* the love between the elderly couple is about old age and sadness. Thomas Pynchon said of the novel in the

New York Times Book Review, "It could be argued that this is the only honest way to write about love, that without the darkness and the finitude there might be romance, erotica, social comedy, soap opera—all genres, by the way, that are well represented in this novel—but not the Big L. What that seems to require, along with a certain vantage point, a certain level of understanding, is an author's ability to control his own love for his characters, to withhold from the reader the full extent of his caring, in other words not to lapse into drivel."

VA : I want to return to the topic of sin, which we touched upon earlier—specifically, salvation through sin.

IS : That's the domain of antinomianism, a recurrent movement in every major religion of Western civilization, and one I've been quite interested in for some time. The extraordinary idea behind it might be reduced to a simple axiom: evil fosters good.

In the Middle Ages, there were Christian sects that endorsed sexual promiscuity as a way to test human freedom and divine love. In Protestantism, the Anabaptists also believed that morality was relative. In the United States, the stories of Anne Hutchinson's rebelliousness and banishment in the mid-seventeenth century and also the episode of the witches of Salem are connected with this current. Sexual apostasy was often an excuse to impose control based on a monolithic view of morality. Ultimately, there is a connection between this type of religious dissidence and Gnosticism.

In Judaism there's a similar trend. Gershom Scholem, in his studies of Sabbateanism, the messianic movement led by

Jacob Frank that ended in ridicule in the seventeenth century, discusses its aftermath: antinomianism. Antinomians believe that the laws of morality aren't absolute; instead, they are applicable depending on context. What is more, a connection with the concept of Edom might be found. *Edom* is a Hebrew term used to refer to the Semitic people who lived in the Negev and who, according to the Bible, descended from Esau. In rabbinical response, the word is used to refer to Christianity, in particular to the Byzantine Empire, just as *Ismaelite* refers to the followers of Islam. *Edomite* might be used as a metaphor for a loose, idol-worshipping person. Scholem says, "Edom symbolizes the unbridled flow of life which liberates man because its force and power are not subject to any law. . . . It was necessary to abolish and destroy the laws, teachings, and practices which constrict the power of life, but this must be done in secret; . . . it was essential outwardly to assume the garb of the corporeal Edom, i.e., Christianity . . . [but] Jesus of Nazareth was no more than the husk preceding and concealing the fruit, who was Frank himself [the reincarnation of Sabbatai Zevi]."

VA : Is there a hell in Judaism?

IS : Not really. There's *Gehenna,* a kind of waiting room where the souls are purified on their way to the World to Come, the *Olam Habah.* It isn't a destination but a transitory stage where, according to rabbinical sources, no one stays for more than twelve months. And there's the *sheol* (meaning "above the dead"), a type of underworld, although it doesn't have a threatening function. There are references to it in Genesis 37–35, Psalm 5–7, and Ecclesiastes 9:5–10. For instance, "the dead know nothing; they have no further reward, and even the memory of them is forgotten," and "whatever your hand finds to do, do it with all your might, for in the grave *[sheol]*, where you are going, there is neither working nor planning nor knowledge nor wisdom." The Christian concept of hell is a far more effective component in reward-and-punishment theology. As is clear from Dante's *Divine Comedy,* it has a different function than that of purgatory.

VA: How so?

IS: One doesn't get out of hell. Purgatory is temporary, a site for penance for those souls capable of reaching heaven.

Personally, I find the idea of a self-selecting group sent to hell quite attractive. Paradise seems like an unappealing destination, replete with "good souls." It's the rebellious ones, the discontent, who make far more interesting company. Don't you think?

Since the Enlightenment, hell has been a metaphor for terrible sites, like Hitler's Auschwitz and Stalin's Siberia. In the existential philosophy—as suggested by Jean-Paul Sartre in his play *No Exit*—hell is "the others."

VA: Do sinful lovers have a place in Dante's hell?

IS: He reserves the second circle for "carnal sinners who subordinate reason to desire." In other words, it's the locus of lust. Virgil points Dante in the direction of a number of recognizable figures driven there by sex and romance, including Cleopatra,

Tristan, Helen of Troy, the Assyrian queen Semiramis, Paris, Achilles, and Dido, queen of Carthage.

VA: In *On Borrowed Words* you speak unabashedly about your sexual awakening as a teenager in Mexico.

IS: It was a rite of passage.

VA: In the memoir, you eventually go to Israel, where you lived for a while before settling in the United States.

IS: In Israel I was in love with a woman, Revital. I lived in a kibbutz not far from Tiberias, near Lake Kineret. Revital was engaged. She was also enlisted in the army. We spent together her last few weeks before she returned to her military post. Those were blissful days.

VA: Was that relationship sinful?

IS: Yes, insofar as Revital was betrothed to another man. But she was taking advantage of her last remaining moments before the wedding.

VA: Did you feel guilty?

IS: There was an element of danger in our encounters. Her future husband wasn't in the area, but news of our liaison could easily reach him.

VA: Do you regret it?

IS: Not in the least. I look back at our intimate moments with affection. We were young. Isn't youth about experimentation?

VA: Were there consequences?

IS: Not for me. As I tell it in *On Borrowed Words,* in the end Revital left me. For years I visualized her in the battlefield. Is she alive? I don't know. I might have received a letter from her, maybe two. I might have written to her as well. But in the end it was better to let things die.

VA: Let's move on to pornography . . .

IS: It's a ubiquitous ingredient of consumer culture, one testing the limits of free expression. The body becomes a marketable item, sheer merchandise. What kind of person makes pornography? Someone desperate for money and with little regard for the mysteries of the body. The more serious question is who consumes pornography? The answer is simple: everyone. Its influence is such that even while keeping away from actual pornographic magazines, videos, toys, Internet sites, and so on, we're defined by it through movies, advertising, and fashion. Look around: our mannerisms have become more explicit. Emphasizing our sexual desires is part of being modern.

VA: How should *pornography* be defined?

IS: It comes from a Greek term via the mid-nineteenth-century French concept of *pornographos,* the art of writing about prostitutes. Suetonius was the master of it. Today the word has a double meaning: it refers to sexually explicit material intended to arouse the consumer (films, magazines, videos, literature, and so on), and also to the industry that produces it.

VA: It's said that pornography begins at the edge of a culture's decorum.

IS: And the limits of our culture, whether geographical or psychological, are inescapably political. Pornography has a right to exist. It's required that it exists for our concept of free speech not to be curtailed. But is there anything pleasing—and I'm using the term in the aesthetic sense—about it? When I was young, my friends and I would buy a copy of *Playboy*. It was a teenage sport, so to speak. At the time the images featured in the magazine were rather tame compared to the limits of pornography today. I would argue that, in their containment, they were less pornographic than erotic: naked women in inviting poses. The extremes we've reached—mechanical intercourse—have deprived the field of any vestige of charm. Not long ago I came across a defense of pornography as we know it now by a prominent feminist cultural critic.

VA: A woman?

IS: Yes. She invited the reader to find the eloquence in pornography and suggested that the genre is astute about itself, recognizing that audiences are drawn to it because sexuality within our social conventions is a prison built on conformity with a stratum of frustration. The effects pornography unravels and the unrestrained desire it generates have an element of utopianism to them. Indeed, there might be some truth to this argument. But at its base pornography isn't only voyeurism without satisfaction but the absolute negation of love. For when a sexual encounter is portrayed as a mechanical tête-à-tête, it isn't about two people finding each other but about refuting their individuality. There isn't plenitude in pornography, only platitude. There's no hope, only sadness. The longing it expresses is a debasement, a loss, a refutation of life.

VA: Is it a sickness?

IS: Yes, a modern sickness. There are comic strips and websites devoted to Walt Disney porno: Snow White having sex with the Seven Dwarves, the Little Mermaid engaging in fellatio. There's also a site that features Barbie and Ken experimenting with positions from the *Kama Sutra*.

VA: Might a cure be found?

IS: I don't think so. The presence of eroticism in the public realm, on the other hand, isn't a loss but a triumph. Think of erotic cinema, for instance. It invites us to perceive the world in a new, provocative way. But eroticism is about discovery, whereas pornography is about repetition, about a sense of déjà vu. What pornography does is repeat sexual scenes while emptying them of any emotional content.

VA: Is there any wisdom in pornography?

IS: The wisdom of boredom. It is the result of solitude, depravation, despair. Yes, pornography is lovelessness. It's a realm where the sexual encounter becomes a sheer technicality, a spilling of juices without incantation. In short, it's love without poetry. Eroticism is alluring because it is mysterious. Think of Robert Herrick's famous eulogy "Upon the Nipples of Julia's Breast":

Have ye beheld (with much delight)
A red rose peeping through a white?
Or else a cherry (double grac'd)
Within a lily centre plac'ed?
Or ever mark'd the pretty beam,

A strawberry shows half-drown'd in cream?
Or seen rich rubies blushing through
A pure smooth pearl and orient too?
So like to this, nay all the rest,
Is each neat nipple of her breast.

What's a nipple? A red rose on a white background, a cherry, a strawberry over ice cream—all that and more that is beyond language, a mystery to be explored through desire.

VA : What are taboos for?

IS : To be broken. Pornography is all about breaching borders, defying limits, being offensive.

VA : What is so threatening about being offended? When I was last in Madrid I came across a book written by Miguel Lorente Acosta, a forensic doctor, entitled *Mi marido me pega lo normal* (My Husband Beats Me as Much as Expected). It immediately brought to mind a time when I was interpreting at a battered women's shelter and the psychologist asked a woman why her husband beat her. The woman replied, "¿Será porque me quiere?"—Could it be because he loves me?

IS : The lover's pathology: he offends me, thus he desires me. He beats me, therefore I'm valuable.

VA : Aggression is an essential part of love.

IS : In the secrecy of the lover's space, it's the line separating affection from hostility.

VA: I wonder what the history is behind the expression *making love*.

IS : A fascinating question. There are references to it in Charles

Dickens, Jane Austen, George Eliot, and George Bernard Shaw, to name a few nineteenth-century British and Irish authors. But how far back does it go? It isn't present in Shakespeare, for instance. I read somewhere that the transition from Mantegazza's original Italian book *Gli amori degli uomini,* published in 1885, to its English translation in 1953, *The Sexual Relations of Mankind,* marks a defining moment—the old *ars amatoria* was cast aside in favor of a new *scientia sexualis.* Calling lovemaking "sexual intercourse" made it seem more controlled and allowed it to be studied, measured, and quantified in a way that the elusive "love" could not.

The English verb *to make* has multiple uses. The *OED* devotes seven pages to it. In general, it means "to cause to exist, to happen, to bring about, to become, to compel, to institute." Semantically, its essence, clearly, is connected with the idea of procreation. The sense is that, through a physical encounter, the lovers "produce" love. There is also "to make war," which, I guess, could be an antonym. To make love is to engage in amorous caressing; also, it means to have sexual intercourse.

VA : It seems cruel to me . . .

I S : That a mere sexual encounter might be described as love? Maybe there's some optimism in the expression. Keep in mind that the informality with which sexual intercourse takes place today is a rather recent development. The beatniks of the 1960s are surely among the most daring generations in human history. They brought down ethical mores in less time than the Greeks succeeded in the siege of Troy.

VA : Has society as a whole become more promiscuous?

IS : Yes, and also more casual.

VA : You've mentioned the Marquis de Sade . . .

IS : The word *sadism* is his legacy, much as *masochism* invokes nineteenth-century author Leopold von Sacher-Masoch, who wrote the novel *Venus in Furs.*

VA : Sade seems to fascinate you.

IS : Just as he did scores of others, including Pierre Klossowski, Simone de Beauvoir, Theodor Adorno, and Octavio Paz. I see him as a prophet of anarchy. Like few others, Donatien Alphonse François, as he was known, tested the conventions of his age. He was a product of the Enlightenment. His views on freedom and responsibility are unique, for he wasn't just a libertine—he applied his actions to a philosophy of life whose impact on contemporary society is enormous. His books *Juliette, The 120 Days of Sodom,* and *Philosophy in the Bedroom* are replete with blasphemy, rape, torture, and an opposition to organized religion.

VA : Was he an antinomian?

IS : No, and not a gnostic either. Sade didn't believe in salvation—he was a fanatic.

VA : An anarchist, in your view, must also endorse some sort of hierarchy.

IS : Yes, and Sade's perversity was not without limits. Its engine was pleasure at any cost and without regard to pain. Indeed, he believed that sex without pain is like food without taste. He abused prostitutes, had an affair with his wife's sister, organized big orgies, and used poison. He also ran for office and endorsed a clear far-left ideological position. In fact, his endurance emerged from his understanding of the interface between the private and public realms. To what degree is a citizen fully free to act as he wishes? Remember: Sade was born in 1740 and died in 1814, as the Napoleonic Wars were winding down.

VA: Did Sade embrace pain even if it brought about death?

IS: Sure. In his last will, Sade described himself thus: "Imperious, choleric, irascible, extreme in everything, with a dissolute imagination the like of which has never been seen, atheistic to the point of fanaticism, there you have me in a nutshell . . . Kill me again or take me as I am, for I shall not change." His lesson remains admirable.

VA: In what sense?

IS: His lesson is admirable in that it fostered the culture of satisfaction we embrace today. Are we all that different from him? Only by degree.

VI

FOR LOVE OF COMMUNITY

VA: Let's focus on community.

IS: In Latin, love of community is *amor humanitatis*. I mentioned
the Greek word *storge*, affection. Love of family is the first
stage in which we're able to recognize that we're surrounded
by and in need of others. Childhood is about trust and kinship. Kinship is a relationship based on blood, marriage, or
adoption. It's at the core of the concept of family, which is defined by natural affiliation.

VA: How so?

IS: As Italians like to say, when the family calls, there's no choice.
We're stuck with it. We pick our friends and drop them, too.
But our relatives are ours forever. That is why family love is
one of the most challenging forms of affection.

VA: Aren't all types of love to some extent public?

IS: This is true insofar as the individual is engaged emotionally with someone else. There's an essential difference between romantic love and sexual encounters on the one hand and kinship and camaraderie on the other. Romantic and sexual love aspire to an exclusive physical union. The lover wants from the loved one full commitment. The rest of the world is part of their relationship only by exclusion. One could claim that these types of love are symptoms of our ingrained need not to be alone in the universe. Loving is a courageous act based on the desire to share one's solitude, to be alone but not lonely. Kinship and camaraderie, on the other hand, place the individual firmly in the social sphere.

VA : Are our social skills innate?

IS : The family forms a nucleus of support in which the person learns to interact with others.

VA : How does storge evolve?

IS : Eventually, as we mature, storge becomes love of community. The recognition that we aren't alone and that others are equally valid is what socialization is about. This recognition is achieved through the family, school, religion, sports, and so on. Friendship is also about love, but not of the physical kind. We long to be in the company of those we love, not because we seek to possess them but because their presence lightens our existence. Friendship is about empathy, cooperation, and understanding. It's about the joining of the self with the cosmos in spiritual ways.

VA : In *On Borrowed Words,* you offer a portrait of your immediate family in Mexico through the prism of language: your father, Abraham Stavans, a TV and stage actor; your mother, Ofelia, a psychologist; your brother Darián, a musician; and your sister Liora, a psychotherapist. The ones taking up most of the space are your father and brother.

IS : Kinship is the prime articulator of our galaxy of emotions. From the father and mother the child learns what love is: to be cared for, to be protected, to have a place of one's own in the world. The autobiography has become a trap. It's designed nowadays as a display of fortitude, but it quickly becomes proof of how the individual is able to overcome misery. Look how much I've suffered, cries the autobiographer, and to what extent I've redeemed myself. It's too bad that the confessional has taken over the tradition, particularly in the United States, a nation that prides itself on individualism. Alcohol, domestic violence, sexual abuse . . . everybody is a survivor! Personally, what interests me in the genre is something else: the need for the self to articulate its own narrative, to make sense of the world. Memory plays an important role, but so does the imagination, for a memoir, in the end, is a carefully constructed lie. In writing about my immediate family, my quest was to understand the way literature, drama, and music shaped our understanding of who the family members are.

VA : Love of others goes hand in hand with selflessness.

IS : Selflessness is a challenging concept. Hillel, the Talmudic scholar, stated (as articulated by the tractate Pirkei Abbot) that the man who puts his talents to selfish uses commits spiritual suicide. I think of the Talmud as the source where the philosophy of selflessness is developed with clarity.

VA: Yet, ironically, the Talmud brought enemies to the Jews.

IS: Yes, based on misinformation. The Talmud was perceived by medieval Christian thinkers as the devil's instrument.

VA: You've also mentioned another Greek word: *philia*, friendship.

IS: Friendship is the most curious of all forms of love. There is no physical aspect to it. And, as I suggested earlier on, it's ruled not by fate but by choice. Nothing is more rewarding than nurturing a lifelong friendship.

VA: Do you have many such friends?

IS: Probably three or four.

VA: Are they male?

IS: Mostly, but not always. Friendship has an admirable quality: it gracefully zooms in and out. Some friends we don't see for years, yet we know they're available whenever we need them.

VA: How does friendship evolve?

IS: Through trust and recognition. A person becomes a friend only after a sense of comfort and familiarity has been established.

VA: Are there models in literature?

IS: There are an excess of models, although they present themselves to us with caveats. Don Quixote and Sancho—can they be friends when there's an economic relationship between them? The same goes for Diderot's Jacques and his master. And it's brain-rattling to ponder the variety of friends in Shakespeare. Bolingbroke in *Richard II* says, "I count myself in nothing

else so happy / As in a soul remembering my good friends"
(2.3.46–47). Claudio, in *Much Ado about Nothing,* says,
"Friendship is constant in all things / Save in the office and
affairs of love" (2.1.166–167). And, of course, one mustn't forget Rosencrantz and Guildenstern.

Over the years, I've found that the wisest, least pedantic of
essayists, the one finding the right balance between philosophy and literature, is Michel de Montaigne. I often read his
work for solace and inspiration, but also for clarity and conviction. In his essay "Of Friendship," Montaigne, in the sixteenth
century, points out that, unlike family, the friends we have in
life are the product of a selection process. While they might
not owe us anything, or vice versa, a sense of loyalty develops.
How to explain then the love between friends? It isn't physical
but spiritual, playing out at the level of companionship. Alone-
ness isn't a natural state. By definition, people seek others.
They seek trust in unformalized fashion. Montaigne states in
Florio's translation of 1603, "Friendship is enjoyed according
as it's desired, it's neither bred, nor nourished, nor increaseth
but in jovissance, as being spirituall, and the minde being refined by use custome."

VA : Do you recall a formative friendship?

I S : Yes. I'll relate to you an anecdote about friendship as an interface of loyalty, religion, and sports. It shows the extent to
which Montaigne is right. Not too long ago I told my ten-year-
old son, Isaiah, this story on the three-hour drive to our summer house in Wellfleet, Cape Cod. He liked one word I kept

repeating: *cascarita*. Here's the story as I remember it: In 1974, during the World Cup, Licho and Javi were our neighbors in Copilco, a middle-class neighborhood in Mexico City close to the Universidad Nacional Autónoma de México (UNAM), the largest university in the country. Copilco is not far from Coyoacán, where Frida Kahlo and Diego Rivera used to live. The barrio's street names made reference to the various disciplines taught at the UNAM; our home was on Calle Odontología. And a block away in the other direction was a park. I was told that Hernán Cortés, en route to Tenochtitlán, stopped in Copilco to water his horses. Who knows? The park had an old fountain that was now just a place where polluted rainwater accumulated and children caught tadpoles.

Licho and Javi aren't their real names. It isn't that I want to hide their identity—I've really forgotten what they were called. I never knew their last name, either. Licho was fourteen when the story takes place, Javi twelve. My brother Darián and I were about the same: thirteen and twelve. Licho wanted to be Germany's Franz Beckenbauer, and I used to pretend I was the Netherlands' star Johann Cruyff. I forget who Darián and Javi's international players of choice were. At any rate, we were all generic kids.

Licho and Javi were late additions to the neighborhood. They were originally from Monterrey, but something had happened—perhaps their parents had divorced or one of them had died—and they were now staying at their grandfather's in Calle Medicina. Whatever the circumstances, the two boys showed up one afternoon in the park. As always, Darían and I were playing impromptu soccer games called *cascaritas*. When Licho and Javi, also avid soccer fans, introduced themselves, we talked about the latest game aired on TV. Not only did they know the score, but Javi was able to quote from memory the entire roster for both teams, the players' jersey numbers, and who had scored a goal in what minute of which game.

Neither Darián nor I was tall, but Licho and Javi were even shorter. After a few cascaritas they invited us for a glass of water at their grandfather's place. The grandfather and his young wife received us warmly and even asked us to stay and eat with them. We kindly said no, for it was time for us to go home. I don't think the fact that we were Jewish was ever mentioned.

As time went by, the friendship grew. After school we met regularly in the park to play yet another mini-game. They liked us, we liked them. But there was something foreign, unexplained in the relationship. It took me years to understand that larger issues such as class and religion were infringing upon us in ways we were utterly unaware of.

Once, while Darián and I waited for Licho and Javi, another neighbor showed up. He was a slim boy who lived in an apartment building not too far away. He got off his bike, and soon enough the three of us were playing. We were expecting Licho and Javi to join us, but they never came. A couple of days later we found out that they had seen us with someone else and had decided not to disturb us.

Why hadn't they joined us? The answer, I came to believe, was jealousy. We were spending time with another neighbor, not with them, an act they interpreted as treason.

I also remember inviting Licho and Javi for dinner once. It must have been a Saturday night, because on Shabbat the family generally spent time together. We had tamales with beans. Licho and Javi were unusually quiet. After dinner, when we had already left the table and gone back to Darián's and my bedroom, Javi seemed to be asking for proof that we were Jewish. I didn't quite understand.

"Your family is Jewish, isn't it?"

I answered yes.

He asked, "How can I know?"

I said I didn't know. We were Jewish, that's all.

"What does that mean?"

"We don't mix meat and dairy products. We go to synagogue. We have a different calendar."

He wanted to know more. I answered as best I could. But he insisted on seeing some evidence.

"Do you want to see our candelabrum?"

He said yes. I brought the menorah that was usually stored in the studio. I also brought a prayer book. He inspected them.

Javi asked if it was true that Jews were disloyal. I didn't know what he meant. The conversation moved to other topics, and soon the four of us ended up playing a board game, I believe.

In any case, over the following summer months we saw each other frequently. One day, Javi announced that their grandfather had won tickets in a raffle, or perhaps someone had given them to him, but whatever it was there were five tickets for the classic soccer match at Estadio Azteca between the ultimate rival teams in Mexican *futbol,* Cruz Azul and América.

The following Sunday, with a few pesos in our pockets to buy food and a souvenir, my brother and I went to Licho and Javi's house. The game was at noon, and the stadium wasn't too far from our neighborhood, but traffic was atrocious when there was a game so we got there early. Their grandfather's car was hardly new, but I noticed that he drove it as if it were a Mustang. Licho, Darián, and I were in the back seat, and Javi was riding shotgun. We were driving at about forty-five miles per hour on Avenida Universidad when the accident happened. I remember it like this: out of the blue there was a person wanting to cross the street, and my guess is that the grandfather didn't see him. In any event, suddenly the man was in front of the car. The grandfather should have hit the brake. Maybe he did, but not in my recollection. We all heard a loud noise and felt a thump.

We immediately understood what had happened and were in shock. What's amazing is that the grandfather never had the intention of stopping the car and helping the victim. Rather, he stepped on the gas. We quickly left the scene of the accident, and when Licho, Darián, and I looked over our shoulder, we could see the body in the distance. The man was in a pool of blood. One leg was on top of the other.

Silence descended. The rest of the drive to the Estadio

Azteca felt like an eternity. I was dizzy and thirsty; Darián was sweating and his hand was grabbing my knee. I may not remember everything that happened, but I do remember that when we were near the parking lot, Javi turned around and said, "What we've witnessed should remain a secret forever. Not a word should come out from anyone in this car." Then he added with a sarcastic tone, or what appeared to me to be one, "Don't let your Jewish self betray you."

v a : What happened at the match?

i s : My imagination has convinced me that América won after much tension, maybe by a single *gol*. When the game was over, Licho and Javi were angry at us for supporting the winning team. They said the game wasn't fair because the referee had favored América. At one point, as we were heading out, Javi pushed me.

When Darián and I returned home, I told him we shouldn't tell our parents what had happened because Licho and Javi's grandfather could be sent to jail. We promised to keep the secret. Neither Darián nor I broke our promise.

The story takes a tragic turn at this point. Darián and I avoided going back to the park to play our cascaritas. My instinct tells me that Licho and Javi didn't go back either. Weeks went by, and we put the incident behind us. September came and with it the beginning of classes. One day we walked by Licho and Javi's house and were surprised to find it empty.

When I asked my mom about it, she took a deep breath and said that a neighbor had told her that at the end of August Javi had suddenly disappeared. One day he walked out of the house, and no one could find him. A search took place and the police got involved. Javi was eventually found, alone and shivering, living under a bridge about a mile away from our neighborhood. His father took him back to Monterrey. Licho stayed a week longer, then he went to Monterrey, too. My mom was also told that the grandfather had fallen ill and been taken to the hospital, but no one knew which one. His wife hadn't been seen in the house, so the whole thing was a big mystery.

VA: The friendship came to an end, then.

IS: It did, in a dramatic fashion. The four of us had developed trust. There was love between us. I'm still able to see Licho and Javi's mestizo faces.

VA: Yet there were plenty of differences between you.

IS: We were Caucasian, of Polish descent. The fact that our family was Jewish seemed to have bothered them, although I never fully understood the nature of Javi's queries.

VA: Did you ever see them again?

IS: When I told Isaiah the story, I added a coda: Years later, during a trip to Miami, I was in a Brazilian restaurant when all of a sudden I seemed to recognize the face of the person seated at a table nearby. It took me a while to see that in his mature gestures there was a trace of a youthful Licho. When I heard him speak Spanish to the young lady with him, I knew for sure. I gathered all the courage I could muster and introduced myself. His amazement was equal to mine, but we managed to exchange pleasantries. I thought I wouldn't be able to ask anything else, but it was he who inquired about Copilco, Darián, and my parents. I soon did the same.

VA : What did he say?

I S : He said Javi lived in Monterrey, was divorced, and had no children. Licho had returned to Mexico City with his fiancée and was studying medicine. He also said his grandfather had died at the hospital while Javi was living under the bridge.

VA : The park makes me think of an aspect of love you haven't touched on: Nature.

I S : With a capital N, the way it was spelled in the nineteenth century. Spinoza is our central interpreter of *de amore natura.* Nature for him was everything, not only trees and animals. The love we have for it is the product of rational thinking. But nature has been turned into something else lately: a fetish.

VA : In what sense?

I S : The advance of our postindustrial society affects the natural order. In response, people develop a nostalgia for the lost order.

VA : Is that bad?

I S : It has obvious grounding in our survival instinct. The more that natural resources are depleted, the less capable we are in finding balance with the environment. The concept of nature as a temple was used by the Argentine-British naturalist and ornithologist W. H. Hudson in a novel called *Green Mansions: A Romance of the Tropical Forest,* published in 1904. The novel was a forerunner of the ecological movement that flourished in the United States and Europe in the 1980s. One of its protagonists, Rima, a kind of female version of Rudyard

Kipling's Mowgli (*The Jungle Book* appeared in 1894), speaks to animals. There's a movie based on it with Anthony Perkins and Audrey Hepburn.

VA : How does the garden fit in with our love of nature?

I S : The garden as a venue for sensual encounters is a legacy of Al-Andalus, in medieval Spain. Arab culture of the time approached the castle within a garden—such as the Alhambra in Granada—as an attempt to implement order in nature. It's also a venue for contemplation and a microcosm of the human psyche. The idea connects to Spinoza's *amor Dei intellectualis,* the love of the divine through nature, about which I talked before.

Medieval Arab and Hebrew poetry was about contemplation, about love and wine. When I think of it I think of *ghazals.* The ghazals produced during the period, written by Arabic and Hebrew poets, use metonymy and exude sensuality. They sing to homosexual love, to wine, to pleasure, and to the encounter between the poet and the divine. The ghazals, also known as *muwashshahat,* are made of brief verses, never more than four to six. They fall into two categories: descriptive and petitionary poems. The descriptive poems concentrate on parts of the beloved's body, such as hair, eyebrows, cheeks, mouth, breasts, waist, and thighs. The petitionary poems focus on a relationship, although the beloved's inner self is never described. In an illustrative poem translated into English by T. Carmi, Moshe ibn Ezra profiles the physical beauty of the lover:

With our imaginary eyes we kiss his lips;
With eyes alone we pluck his beauty's buds;
We sate our eyes on his abundant grace;
Our lips the while are faint with famine's pangs.

Interestingly, the ghazals aren't produced exclusively by men.
Among the most stunning female authors is Wallada bint al-
Mustakfi, whose work is fueled by her love for Ibn Zaidun.
Here is an example, translated by Mona Mikhail:

I am fit for high positions, by
God
And am going my way with pride
. . . .
Forsooth, I allow my lover to
touch my cheek,
And bestow my kiss on him who
craves it.

The senses dwell on nature, and the soul finds peace in it. Our
model of paradise, in biblical terms, is a garden, a place where
balance prevails—natural and human balance. The earthly
gardens are an approximation. Human imperfections are a
component. There's a difference between the garden and the
park: the first is private, intimate, personal; the second is public. Maybe because I was born in a city where gardens were
minuscule, even pathetic, I have a longing for a space where
nature allows for retreat and contemplation. I find bucolic im-

ages of the garden appealing. The park in the neighborhood where I grew up, by contrast, was rather unattractive, although I spent endless afternoons in it playing with friends. I knew it wasn't mine; it belonged to the community—a social space, a site of leisure, dialogue, social recreation. I internalized its function much more.

V A : Was the park also the site of romantic encounters?

I S : I'm afraid not. I wasn't interested in the neighborhood girls. The ones at school were far more enticing.

V A : Did you meet with them outdoors?

I S : I mostly remember exchanging kisses and other caresses in the darkness of movie theaters. It might have been a matter of class. Whereas the Mexican poor make abundant use of parks, especially on weekends, the upper-middle class isolates itself in its own indoor fortresses: athletic facilities, upscale business areas, concert halls. The garden is a venue for sports and picnics. As a result, what interests me about the outdoors is . . . well, the connection between nature and happiness.

V A : Not a secret garden but a public one . . .

I S : I appreciate the garden far better through art. Among my favorite paintings is Pierre-Auguste Renoir's 1881 painting *Le déjeuner des canotiers* (The Luncheon of the Boating Party). Renoir, the impressionist painter and father of the film director Jean Renoir, once said, "Why shouldn't art be pretty? There are enough unpleasant things in the world." In the painting Renoir depicts a splendid scene of outdoor joy in the town of Chatou, on the Seine, a getaway for Parisians of the nineteenth century that was known as a spot for rowing. He portrays a group of people on a balcony at the Maison Fournaise, a place that offered rowing skiffs and other boats for rent and included a hotel and restaurant. Renoir enjoyed the Maison Fournaise and used it in his paintings several times. At times he bartered with his art for lodging and a meal. In a letter to a friend, he stated, "I hope to see you in Paris on the first of October, for I am at Chatou. I'm doing a painting of oarsmen which I've been itching to do for a long time. I'm not getting any younger, and I didn't want to defer this little festivity which later on I won't any longer be able to afford; already it's very difficult. . . . Even if the enormous expenses I'm incurring prevent me from finishing my picture, it's still a step forward; one must from time to time attempt things that are beyond one's capacity."

The individuals included by Renoir in *Le déjeuner des canotiers* are all acquaintances: editors, daughters of entrepreneurs, artists, journalists, sailors, seamstresses, and poets (including, maybe, Jules Laforgue). It's a mix of backgrounds. After the Industrial Revolution, French society of the time was able to enjoy long weekend outings and indulge in an atmosphere of idleness, which, as Catullus appropriately put it in "Carmen 51," brings trouble but also delight and passion. Renoir's work is superb in re-creating the mood of the time. The garden becomes the river bank, where love and friendship are fixtures. Flirting is done casually, without consequence. There lies the power: social interaction has entered another degree of compromise. Conventions have been relaxed, nothing is taken too seriously, and casual encounters define the way people shape their life.

VA : The joy of company . . .

IS : Whereas love of oneself and love of another are sharply focused, love of community is diffuse. The target isn't a person alone but a group and what it represents. Think of butterflies dancing around a bush: their nervous movement is what connects them with the group. They're part of a larger picture.

Walter Benjamin, called by Terry Eagleton "the Marxist Rabbi," who committed suicide in Port Bou, Spain, because he believed the Nazis were about to seize him, devoted a considerable amount of attention to a phenomenon of bourgeois society in the mid-nineteenth century: the arcade, what today we would describe as the mall. Benjamin worked on a project to understand the historical, cultural, and psychological implications of the arcade between 1927 and 1939 but never finished. What remains is an immense pile of notes and commentary. Yet in Benjamin's case the fractured, unfinished nature of the material isn't an exception. He often composed several drafts of an essay. And he pursued ideas only halfway through. I find this quality of his oeuvre—its inconclusiveness—attractive. It is symptomatic of the arcade project that he would fail to complete it. After all, the concept is open-ended: he conceived of the arcade as a series of interconnected hallways, a locus of commerce and divertissement. Benjamin, as a cultural commentator, approached the subject from different perspectives: media, philosophy, fashion, furniture, drugs, architecture, medicine, romance . . .

VA: You have an essay on him in *The Inveterate Dreamer* called "Walter Benjamin: The Demon of Inspiration."

IS: What attracts me the most about Benjamin is his view that everything around us, the entire world, ought to be interpreted. Yet he doesn't offer a set, dogmatic, cookie-cutter theory. He's interested in the metaphysical—for example, the mystical— aspect of culture and opts to understand it from an interdisciplinary perspective. He isn't a consistently clear stylist, but compared to his Frankfurt school admirer Theodor Adorno, who wrote prolifically about a number of topics, particularly the "new" music of Arnold Schoenberg and Alban Berg, Benjamin is accessible. His oscillation between Marxism and Jewishness is emblematic of the dilemma of secular German Jews in the first half of the twentieth century.

VA: You mentioned Benjamin and drugs.

IS: He wrote a lucid essay on eating hashish in Marseilles. And he has related sections in his book *One-Way Street* and in his ambitious yet unfinished arcade project. His interest in drugs was strictly intellectual. He kept a detailed record of his experiences—he called them "protocols"—detailing how his mind functioned under the influence. Not only did he discuss the topic with others (Jean Selz, for instance), but at times he smoked hashish with them. In some ways, Benjamin sought to discover another space inside our mind, a private chamber, where our intellectual capacities are distorted yet the self still functions. Jürgen Habermas, in an essay called "A Generation Apart from Adorno," described Adorno as having "a presence of mind, a spontaneity of thought, a power of formulation that I have never seen before or since. . . . When you were with Adorno you were in the movement of his thought. . . . He lacked the pretensions and the affectations of the stilted and 'autocratic' avant-garde[ist]." The same, I believe, might be said of Benjamin, although his thoughts didn't always emerge fully formed, as if they were already finished.

v a : When I talk to you I feel I'm in the presence of a mind at work, sorting everything out easily, spontaneously, through interpretation.

i s : Curiosity is the fuel that makes a critic active.

v a : Have you ever smoked hashish?

i s : Years ago, in Morocco.

v a : What about other drugs?

i s : In my youth—herbs, not amphetamines. I would describe my involvement with them as limited—a testing of the doors of perception, but not à la Carlos Castaneda.

v a : Do drugs impair a critic's vision?

i s : Or do they expand it? George Steiner, in his autobiography *Errata,* laments not having accepted the invitation he once received to take LSD and wonders about the extent to which his view of literature would have changed. Imagine for a second how much more imaginative, and probably more coherent, some critics would be after experimenting with drugs.

VA: I'm interested in the connection between love and drugs.

IS: Do you mean aphrodisiacs? Love and drugs are, in my view, dissociated realms. The sexual urge can be aroused through jimsonweed, Spanish fly, and mandrake, but, while desire might be convened, a sustained engagement between people involving affection requires a far more elusive ingredient: maturity.

VA: Let's go back to the arcade. Talk about love and commerce, please.

IS: When I was young, Mexico City had numerous stores. But in the last thirty years it has become a gigantic shopping center made of small islands of commerce intersecting with one another—a magisterial arcade. And yet the metropolis, while one of the largest in the planet (its population in 2005 was close to twenty-two million), is in the so-called Third World. It's just another example of the limits of capitalism. Maybe it's because it isn't Europe or the United States that the embrace of the market economy in Mexico is as obvious as it is. It combines the old and the new in equal measure, the irrelevant and the fashionable.

The concept of the "third space" is essential to twenty-first-century capitalism. The home is still a private domain, as is the office, the locus where work is performed. But another space—the store, the cafeteria, the park, the mall—is freer and less conventional. Our understanding of community is defined by the arcade: people become merchandise. The same space was used in the eighteenth century, and after, by the salon. The salon is a symbol of the ancien régime, the domain of women. With the fall of the aristocratic class in Europe and, thus, the decline of the court as a space of social encounter, the salon became an institution in which culture was not merely debated but shaped. Indeed, the female organizers of these salons—Mademoiselle Madeleine de Scudéry, Madame Marie-Thérèse Rodet Geoffrin, and Madame Germaine de Staël, among them—were agents at times of stabilization and at other times of change. The salons included a display of exquisite dishes and elegant fashion. More important, these salons were showcases of manners. People of the bourgeoisie in places like Paris and Vienna gathered for the sheer art of seeing and being seen. The *salonièrs* were at center stage, orchestrating every single aspect of the event, from the guest list to the performers (musicians, actors, and so on) to the topic of conversation. They were muses. The salons would often take place once a week, at a fixed time. Their glamour depended on word of mouth and on a core group of guests, bons vivants as well as the great conversationalists known as *causeurs* whose reputation spread by word of mouth. It's crucial to view these events as the expression of an increasingly influential bourgeoisie, whose fingerprints would eventually be seen on every aspect of life, from politics to sexuality, from poetry to cuisine. Egalitarianism was the principal motif behind the effort. And love in this context was a performance. How one behaved, how one spoke, how one conducted oneself at every step, from the moment of arrival at the salon until departure, mattered. In a sense, the collision between the domestic and the public is exemplified: the realm was the household, but an elite of habitués was invited in.

The arcade, instead, is about being on the move. It's about sight as well but in a more dynamic fashion. Consumers in a mall talk, but they also walk, eat, and buy. Or, to use contemporary jargon, they "just hang out."

VA : What's the etymology of the word *arcade*?

IS : The term is French, with Italian roots, *arcata,* from the Latin *arcus.* It refers to a series of arches supported by columns, piers, and pillars, either freestanding or attached to a wall, to form a gallery.

VA : The arcade makes me think of the French word *voyeur.*

IS : The word *voyeurism* has come to be understood as a perversion: to indulge oneself by means of images, especially of an obscene type. The voyeur, in clinical psychology, is a person who looks at others naked or performing sexual acts in order to find pleasure. But in French the word *voyeur* is less charged. It simply refers to an observer. The arcade is a magisterial salon, a promenade where people parade themselves. Looking and speaking are the primary activities. Fashion, conversation, shopping, as well as visual and culinary entertainment, are all important features.

VA : The arcade serves as a meeting place . . .

IS : Yes, it's the site for a gathering, a get-together, a rendezvous, a soirée. It's a more open, democratic place than the salon, a venue where what matters is what's current, where money buys everything: food, clothes, dreams, happiness, and security. It would be easy to describe it as a mirage, but it isn't: the key to the mall's longevity is its constant mutability. Colors, sounds, smells, tastes, and touches are always transitory. Nothing lasts. In this sense, the mall is the place to put oneself up for sale.

The photographs of artist Daniela Rossell might be among the best to have captured the spirit of the mall, albeit indirectly. Her book *Ricas y famosas,* published in 2002, was seen, as one critic put it, as "a bombshell . . . irreverent, sexy, kitsch, grotesque" in her native Mexico. Rossell spent years photographing rich women in their environment: palatial houses with ornamented bedrooms filled with stuffed animals, rococo living rooms with zebra-themed upholstery, decadent swimming pools . . . Rossell's characters, in their costumes, with layers upon layers of plastic surgery, are equally artificial. The viewer gets the sense that nature has been exiled from the Mexican ruling class; or better, that nature has been domesticated to such a degree as to become a museum.

One particular image, "La niña y la sirvienta," depicts a rich, flashy young lady, barefoot, wearing a tight metallic dress and reclining on a sofa. She is in a large, Moorish-style room filled with stuff: a Persian rug, silk-upholstered sofas, matching pillows, objets d'art, golden plates and cups on the table. The room is designed in the colors brown, orange, and maroon. To the right of the young lady is the housemaid. The two of them are looking at us. Their facial expressions are flat, mechanical. The shot is taken looking down at the room from the balustrade on the second floor. What's powerful is Rossell's atmosphere. This is what the nouveau riche are about, she tells us. Consumerism today has given place to a class not unlike the aristocracy surrounding Marie Antoinette in eighteenth-century France: excessive, self-denying, disconnected.

The mall is an emblem of that attitude, even though its clientele is the middle class. It emerges like an oasis in the desert, ignoring the social contradictions around it. Its statement is straightforward: material possession is everything. The mall focuses on how you look, who you are with, what you eat, how you keep up with the times, how many credit cards are in your wallet . . . You need to be in constant change, to revamp your look at all times. The mall is the garden of earthly delights.

Entering the Mall of America, in Bloomington, Minnesota, is not unlike being transported to a fantasy à la Jonathan Swift, except in reverse, in which Gulliver becomes a miniscule being. And have you ever entered a mall when it's closed? It's difficult to come up with a more depressing image, because the mall's furniture is people. Visitors bring it to life. When they are absent, the place looks dreadful: stores are closed, escalators are still, neon lights have a depressive quality to them. Worse, there's a pervasive silence that covers the place, which emphasizes the degree to which our lives are made of noise. Busy people, like bees, produce noise at all times and are also surrounded by it. Without the buzzzzz, who are we? In addition, the mall's management makes sure there's music—better,

Muzak—in the background at all times: Barry Manilow, the Bee Gees, Gloria Gaynor, Paul Anka, Barbra Streisand, whatever not-so-fashionable performer is deemed appropriate to fill in the space. There might also be a digital soundtrack making the environment more palatable: birds, crickets, waves, the wind . . . Next time you enter a mall sit at a busy intersection and appreciate the noise. It's a symphony of human vanity.

VA: Does commerce alter our emotions?

IS: It channels them. Take the Hallmark greeting card. You find a Hallmark section in supermarkets and drugstores, as well as convenience, stationery, and office-supply stores, and so on. In other words, the card is ubiquitous. How to conceptualize the artifact? It might be a stretch, but in its basic design, it's a folded piece of literature that intertwines graphics with one-line maxims. The connection between the two forms of communication offers humor and folk wisdom about age, time, money, and relationships. Greeting cards rotate around calendar dates: birthdates, anniversaries, holidays, and special occasions. Why have they become important? The answer is straightforward. Ours is perceived to be an era in which the individual is disengaged and self-consumed. Hallmark stresses the importance of superficial contact.

VA: Today, the media multiplies images of sexuality and romance.

IS: It also degrades them. Not long ago, I saw on TV a lover who proposed to his fiancée during a Red Sox game at Fenway Park. Does the man who proposes on the screen at a baseball game hold up his love for all to scrutinize so that his love is validated by the public? Or does he cheapen the most intimate question by placing it after an ad for trucks or hot dogs, and avoiding the direct and intimate communication between lovers?

V A : What about the Internet?

I S : The Internet offers a variation on the theme of romance and media. I spent about ten minutes observing a singles chat room, and I think there are important differences between the chat room and the matchmaking website. The chat room allows people to meet, whereas the matchmaking site is specifically designed to find a mate. In any case, the Internet has utterly revolutionized our understanding of love. Matchmaking sites are the modern electronic salon. Such sites promise to be a meeting place and a clearinghouse for those seeking romance. They promise to be the fertile ground for future unions. Here love is quick and compatibility guaranteed. The prevalence of these sites exposes a certain postmodern desperation. It's a life conversation, yes, but it's also anonymous.

V A : We've reached, then, a stage in which love might be said to be virtual.

I S : Yes, although in my view there isn't reason to worry: virtual love will never substitute the tête-à-tête. But the classified section of newspapers, the one devoted to lovers' quests, is being pushed aside by its Internet equivalent. In large metropolitan areas, millions of people live side by side, yet they are more alone than ever. Finding a mate isn't easy in the big city. Passersby, forced to make use of every last second of their time, ignore each other on the subway, in the supermarket, outside the school. They look for ways to escape the public eye, to discover others in unexpected realms. The Internet grants the user a sense of anonymity difficult to equate in the non-virtual world. There's also the issue of intimacy. It might appear otherwise, but in contemporary life the spaces available for private, confidential encounters have been drastically minimized. Where do teenage lovers go in search of privacy? An empty corner in the local mall, an abandoned truck left in a backyard, the darkness of a dead-end street late at night, a friend's vacant apartment . . . The pay-per-hour hotels—in Mexico they were called *Hotel Garage*—used to be an option, but these joints are increasingly on the list of endangered species, victims of the market economy.

VA : Has language also adapted to virtual love?

IS : No doubt. Love is less stable, more transitory today. Expressions of affection are as perishable as greeting cards.

A frequent term on the Internet is *portal*. It comes from *portāle,* the city gate in Middle English, Old French, and medieval Latin. It's a door, an entrance, in Internet lingo a website connecting to other sites, which in turn connect to other sites, ad infinitum. I see it as another version of the arcade, a series of interconnected hallways. The Internet is a portal to other dimensions of love that have not yet been explored. Meanwhile, the spaces for intimacy in the modern world, and the patience to remain loyal to one's interest, have been noticeably reduced. It isn't that two people can't find themselves alone in a room. The obstacle is far more complex; it has to do with silence. A couple learns to be together not only by sharing words but by synchronizing their internal silences. It's revealing to listen to the pauses between messages, the quiet that takes place as part of the dialogue in a conversation between older people. That quiet is an essential feature in a person's life, the interstices in which one is able to recapitulate, to reflect, and to ponder. Falling in love isn't only about feelings but about that synchronicity.

VA : In the "Vortices" chapter, you also mentioned love of nation.

IS : It's a malady inherited from the nineteenth century. In order to justify its existence, to articulate its past and define its future, every society shapes its own narrative. The biblical narrative might be seen, sub specie aeternitatis, as a thorny relationship— a love affair—between the divine and the people of Israel. The concept of "the chosen" establishes the parameters of this relationship. There's a uniqueness to it, an exclusiveness. Jacob is mostly referred to in the Bible as Israel; his twelve children are privileged. Their responsibility is to rise above other nations, to claim divine selection by keeping a stricter moral standard.

VA : Yet to love one's own land is natural.

IS : It isn't about real estate but about inheritance: this land is *my* land! I long for a future without anthems and flags, in which people are able to live anywhere.

VA : What about nationalism in the United States?

IS : In the United States, the narrative of nationalism has undergone a series of permutations. One might think of a number of leitmotifs—the concepts of God and nation, for instance—that have served as the social glue. The British settlers believed also that they were chosen, a New Canaan capable of overcoming the deficiencies of the mother country, England. The first places of gathering where the nation defined itself were churches and meetinghouses. In the nineteenth century, with the arrival of the Enlightenment and the spread of secularism, the divine was replaced by another cohesive force: the feeling of a shared destiny. Nathaniel Hawthorne reacted to the Civil War between northern and southern states over slavery by arguing that the war gave him, and others like him, a rationale for embracing the idea of a union. Indeed, that word, *union,* was much in vogue at the time. In that period, as has been argued, the country was United States, not *the* United States; that is, a federal agglomeration of entities and not a single unit. The places of gathering were political forums.

The second half of the twentieth century, and in particular the 1980s, brought another leitmotif: the self. The United States is less a nation than a corporation constituted by millions of self-interests, all joined under one banner: the pursuit of individual satisfaction. Appropriately, the mall is its place of gathering.

I want to stress that the mall isn't a strictly American phenomenon, though. Europe, Asia, and Latin America are infested with them. In Mexico City, where I visit regularly, there are three, sometimes four malls per small neighborhood. I'm not talking about a block with a handful of stores but acres of real estate transformed into temples of egotism.

V A : Love of country, then, is tied to love of self.

I S : The expression "For love of country" has an altruistic ring to it. It encourages sacrifice of the type promoted by average patriots.

V A : Isn't patriotism a form of humanism?

I S : Humanism is another legacy of the Enlightenment. It stresses the belief in universal brotherhood. The world is our home, and it is our duty to protect it, to live in peace and harmony. These ideas are brought down by nationalism.

V A : How so?

I S : In compartmentalizing humankind into units (that is, nations), nationalism stresses not the universal but the regional.

V A : Still, love of country, either as amor humanitatis or as patriotism, is also about home.

I S : Ah, home! Finally we've reached the fountainhead of love. Or have we? Such are the changes in human life in the last one thousand years that the word *home* is totally redefined. It no longer refers to the physical structure where a person dwells but refers, more amply, to "a valued place," as the *OED* states, and also to "an environment offering security and love," a utopia like the one described in *The Wizard of Oz:* "A place where there isn't any trouble. . . . It's not a place you can get to by a boat or a train. It's far, far away. Behind the moon, beyond the rain."

V A : "Close your eyes . . ."

I S : "and tap your heels together three times. And think to yourself, there's no place like home." *The Wizard of Oz* is an extraordinary disquisition on homelessness. What does Dorothy pine for all along? To return to Kansas. Yet her home, at least in the 1939 movie with Judy Garland, is depicted in sepia colors, whereas the Land of Oz is in flashy colors. It's also a place afflicted by tornados. Why does she want to go back? It's simple: because although home might not be an exciting place, it symbolizes love. There lies the appeal of the story: like Ulysses, she's a wanderer.

VA: Is there a difference between patriotism and nationalism?

IS: While the former is simply defined by the *OED* as "love of and devotion to one's country," the latter is an ideology that over-emphasizes patriotism, taking it to an extreme, hence making the love of country into a form of superstition. But what exactly is "love of country," I ask myself. How does one transpose the sentimental connection to others into a loyalty to an abstract entity such as the nation-state? Samuel Johnson was conscious of the absurdity of this duty when he famously defined patriotism as "the last resort of a scoundrel." Ambrose Bierce, in *The Devil's Dictionary,* went one step further: he stated it to be "combustible rubbish read to the torch of any one ambitious to illuminate his name."

For centuries the glue that kept society together was religion. It has been argued that nationalism, as a modern concept, emerged at the time of the French Revolution. It would be useful to trace its origins even further back. It's true that the so-called age of discovery, in the sixteenth century, pushed the Spanish, the Portuguese, and the Dutch beyond their confines into transoceanic realms. Strictly speaking, these were not nations but empires. We see Vasco da Gama in a nineteenth-century watercolor landing in Calicut with a banner of the crown. He set out from Lisbon to Mombassa, in what is Kenya today, and then India, looking for a trade route with the Far East. He was an envoy of King Manuel I of Portugal, who commissioned him to find Christian lands and expand commercial trajectories. Likewise Francisco Pizarro, whose travels across the Atlantic brought him to Peru, where he defeated the Inca Empire. At the time of Pizarro's first expedition, in 1524, Spain was already close to being España, a series of disjointed kingdoms unified by a single religion: Catholicism. At the heart of the nationalist enterprise is not a flag, an anthem, or a shared sense of history—these are afterthoughts. The most important glue behind the concept of nation is faith. In Pizarro's time, the Spanish monarchs, Ferdinand of Aragon and Isabella of Castile, used religion as a unifier to expel the Jews and to fight against the Moors. Other elements came to the fore as well, among them a single language and the cohesiveness of a geographical soil. These factors constitute an early stage of the formation of the nation-state.

v a : In what sense is the love of language connected to nationalism?

i s : In the early nineteenth century, Constantin François de Chasseboeuf, Comte de Volney, said that the first book of a nation is a dictionary of its language, but clearly he was not speaking about the chronology of events, as his statement is not borne out by certain facts, which he would have known: the United

States did not have its own dictionary—Webster's—until 1806, thirty years after it declared its independence from England in 1776. Colonialism uses weapons, money, persuasion, prisons, education, entertainment, and language as the principal tools for the spread of values and moral codes across the globe. Dictionaries often come after the fact, to catalog the reality of a nation already formed. Antonio de Nebrija described language as "siempre la compañera del imperio"—always a companion of empire. Think, for instance, of national anthems. What are these songs we sing with pride? A nation's language becomes a conduit to express pride. Could you imagine the Israeli anthem in Arabic or the American one in German? Not only the music but the words define us.

VA : An anthem is a display of loyalty.

IS : True, and not only in times of crisis. The anthem is a mechanism to ascertain our connection to a place and a group of people. Furthermore, they sublimate one's love of country. *La Marseillaise*—thus named because it was the first song by a band of *fédérés* from Marseille sung in Paris—was composed in 1792, three years after the events at the Bastille. It remains an expression of total devotion, a celebration of camaraderie as a form of sacrifice.

The age of revolution at the end of the eighteenth century gave place to a fever for independence, and soon other emerging nations chose a flag and a set of symbols, and, as time went by, a contest might be organized to identify an anthem.

V A : Even though you went to the Yiddishe Shule, you must have memorized in elementary school, as I did, "Mexicanos al grito de guerra . . . ," Mexicans ready at the call of war.

I S : Was there a choice? It's a behavioral mechanism of the type B. F. Skinner studied.

V A : I always remember that awful baroque sentence, "Mas si osare un extraño enemigo / profanar con su planta tu suelo . . ." (but if a strange enemy dared to desecrate your soil with its foot), made cornier by the use of the -re subjunctive. All Mexican children misinterpreted it; we knew, without a doubt, that Masiosare was one mean stranger who needed to be stopped before he did who knows what mischief to our soil with poison ivy, marijuana, or some other dangerous plant.

I S : Pure jingoism! The image that comes to mind is of a martyred soldier, like the "Niños héroes," the six heroic teenagers—they were children, really—who, rather than die at the hands of the invading American army in 1847, preferred to throw themselves to their death from atop Chapultepec Castle. Well, one of them did. The other five died too, but probably less theatrically. They were immortalized not in an anthem but in a poem by Amado Nervo, which all Mexican children had to memorize. The Mexican anthem, like any other anthem I'm familiar with, makes sure the troops are ready should an enemy invade the country. Love of country isn't about individual choice but about devotion. Edmund Burke said in *Reflections on the Revolution in France* that "to make us love our country, our country ought to be lovely." Patriotism emphasizes the superiority of one's own space through propaganda. It's a cheap, unrefined type of love.

VA: It has evolved, though.

IS: It's the scope that changes. For instance, Giuseppe Garibaldi, who fought for a unified Italy, was a hero. Ernesto "Che" Guevara fought for a continent, and he, too, was a hero. And today a member of al Qaeda is another type of hero, fighting for the supremacy of a belief. The transition goes hand in hand with the recurrent motif of immigration. Nowadays people are on the move for different reasons: economic, religious, political, social . . . What kind of connection do immigrants develop toward the land of arrival? Alienation gives place to acceptance. That acceptance is transformed to fervent nationalism.

VA: And wars are an opportunity to emphasize patriotism.

IS: Wars are patriotic portals. Politicians rally the animosity of their constituency to manufacture consent. And poets from antiquity to the present, like Pindar in his Olympian odes, celebrate the victor's achievement. As soldiers die, love of country becomes more fervent—and fetid, too. Martyrdom and love of country go hand in hand. The word *martyr* has religious connotations. It means sacrificing one's life rather than renouncing religious beliefs. The connection is fitting: nationalism is, to be sure, a form of religion. Nowhere is this connection better exemplified today than in the readiness of fundamentalist Muslims to die for their cause, which is simultaneously their faith and their nationhood.

VA: Of the vortices of love you listed at the outset of our tête-à-tête, love of country is the one about which your opinions seem the most stringent.

IS: It's the only facet I believe we should do without. It's a false portal.

VA: Do you truly believe a future without nations is possible?

IS: Neither possible nor probable. Still, I believe in it. A future without politicians would be a fine substitute. Don't you think?

VA: Why?

IS: Politicians are egomaniacs. Even the most philanthropic make their living stressing the superiority of one group at the expense of others. And they confuse love with allegiance.

VA: I assume you would never run for office.

IS: Actually, I would change the preposition: running *from* office.

VA: I've read that you were part of the Mexican army.

IS: When I was eighteen, like millions of others, I enlisted in it.

VA: Were you ready to die for Mexico?

IS: No.

VA: Why not?

IS: I've always perceived myself as *anational* . . . not atheistic, but *anational.*

VA: You've invented a word.

IS: Isn't it strange that no lexicon includes it? Perhaps it is covered by *stateless,* in Spanish *apátrida.*

VA: Would you be ready to sacrifice yourself for the love of a cause?

IS: Yes.

VA: What cause?

I S : The upholding of intellectual freedom.

V A : And die for it?

I S : What else is left without it? My family comes first, of course.
But the only principle I uphold is the principle to disagree.
And if I can't have it, I'd rather be silent.

V A : Initially, I was doubtful we could reach this far, Ilan.

I S : What do you mean?

V A : You've covered a lot of ground.

I S : The questions have been inspiring.

V A : Love didn't used to seem to me as complex an emotion as you've suggested since we started our dialogue. Have you enjoyed it?

I S : Quite a bit. There's something utterly preposterous in what we set out to achieve: the absolute examination of an emotion, from all possible perspectives. Isn't it like attempting to count grains of sand on the beach? And what do we have to show for our efforts? The one aspect I've enjoyed more than any other relates to intellectual tasks in which I've been engaged in the past. Whatever the objective, I relish applying intelligence in order to make ideas coherent, synthesizing while also reflecting, digesting information in a personalized way, partially, without hiding behind a scientific method. Ideas need to be pondered from all angles. The ideas might not be always original, but the perspective is. When you first proposed the endeavor to me I must say I thought there was something quixotic in it. Love is too abstract, too amorphous a sentiment. Or perhaps, conversely, it's simply a word. At its core our endeavor is ridiculous and maddening.

VA: Did you find it rewarding?

IS: Yes, rewarding too, because the art of conversation is unique and undervalued.

VA: You've talked repeatedly about Socrates.

IS: The ultimate *conversateur.* He believed that knowledge was possible only through absolute definitions. Yet as any lexicographer knows, absoluteness in definition isn't possible. At the core, then, Socrates embraced the impossibility of human knowledge: "I only know I know nothing." That's why he didn't sit down to write a book: oral language is exploratory, ethereal, uncommitted. In conversations and through teaching, I set my mind free, and, in so doing, I rhetorically "wander as I wonder," to use a line by Langston Hughes.

VA: Is the preference for oral explorations a form of modesty?

IS: Not in the least. In fact, I'm convinced there's something dangerous about free expression of ideas of this kind. In recognizing that knowledge is impossible, the teacher refutes his own being.

v a : Yet there's a pleasure in the exploration itself.

i s : Exactly. And that pleasure is my raison d'être. Over the years, as both interviewer and interviewee, I've learned to appreciate the possibilities of such exploration. In an age of instant information, conversation is a casualty. There isn't much time for patient reflection. Unhappily, we seem to define the word *conversation* as a mere exchange of information. A dialogue is much more: an invitation to mature. As you know, I'm a teacher and scholar. Throughout my career, people have identified me as an expert in a wide range of areas. The concept of expertise annoys, maybe even infuriates me. It's an intellectual prison. Why can't a specialist on African tribal dialects also be qualified in quantum physics? Is it absurd to expect that a lawyer focusing on tax law might also find herself at home in the poetry of Seamus Heaney? In an extensive tête-à-tête such as ours, I haven't felt constrained. On the contrary, I've experienced that enviable type of freedom that comes about on lazy summer days when one wanders around looking to entertain one's mind, and then, suddenly, the unexpected happens: a walk in the woods delivers us to a region never seen before, a phone call opens up memories about a relative long forgotten, and so on. At these occurrences, we marvel at the accidental nature of life. Indeed, many of our thoughts are the result of haphazard events. For example, we stumble on a DVD of a Marx Brothers film and, upon watching it, realize it dwells on the topic of tyranny in a more eloquent way than Machiavelli. But then we return to Machiavelli and discover that he defined the topic centuries before in such a subtle fashion that even the Marx Brothers wouldn't exist without him. In any case, scores of questions you've asked in these past months have prompted me to rethink my existential position. Who am I? How did I end up thinking this way? Am I what I think? Descartes's dictum—cogito, ergo sum—is only partially true. What matters isn't that I think, but what I think about. Am I too selfish, only concerned with my own universe and excluding others from it? To what extent do I give myself to others? A quotation from Hillel keeps returning to my mind: "If I'm not for myself, then who will be? If I'm only for myself, then who am I? And if not now, when?" Love encourages us to live the present at its fullest and to overcome our personal isolation to interact with others—not only through words but also through silence. Silence is one of the topics in Ludwig Wittgenstein's philosophy of language as it appears in his *Tractatus Logico-Philosophicus.*

VA: You've written about Wittgenstein in several corners of your work. You mention him in the preface to *The Disappearance.*

IS: I've defined my life in the last few years by his statements that the limit of our language is also the limit of our world and that whatever cannot be said doesn't exist. First and foremost, it's essential to recognize that everything around us, everything we do and think, might be reduced to a morpheme. And if it can't be, then it's because it falls into the realm of the impossible.

VA: In *Dictionary Days* you state that the impossible is whatever exists beyond language.

I S : It might be nothingness.

V A : Why nothingness?

I S : Well, if it's impossible, then it's beyond our speech and, thus, beyond our comprehension. But the impossible isn't what I want us to discuss now. Instead, I'm interested in the possible. Wittgenstein assumed that if something can be said, it exists. He doesn't concern himself with how we say what we say. In my view, when we utter the word *love* we refer to a concrete emotion, a feeling. But the word can be understood in myriad ways within a single language. And when we move into the realm of polyglotism, the possibilities, as I've repeatedly argued to you, are multiplied. *Liebe* in German is different from *amor* in Spanish. In other words, if something can be said it will be said according to a particular context, a set of coordinates in time and space that define that morpheme in a unique way. Granted, some words—words describing not emotions but objects—are more stable. Still, context is everything. What a person in Manhattan on a hectic Monday morning means by the word *clock* is different from what someone in Alexandria, Egypt, meant on another Monday morning, at roughly the same time, in the thirteenth century.

V A : Words are transitional.

I S : They're also a set of conventions. Why is the word *moon* used to describe "the natural satellite of Earth, visible by reflection of sunlight and having a slightly elliptical orbit, approximately 356,000 kilometers (221,600 miles) distant at perigee and 406,997 kilometers (252,950 miles) at apogee"? Why not use, instead, *apple,* or the nonsensical word *pryxtezia?* Our lexicon is entirely fixed yet utterly arbitrary.

Nonsense, after all, isn't chaos but another type of order. Consider Lewis Carroll's poem "Jabberwocky," part of *Through the Looking Glass, and What Alice Found There:*

'Twas brillig, and the slithy toves
Did gyre and gimble in the wabe:
All mimsy were the borogoves,
And the mome raths outgrabe.

"Beware the Jabberwock, my son!
The jaws that bite, the claws that catch!
Beware the Jubjub bird, and shun
The frumious Bandersnatch!"

He took his vorpal sword in hand;
Long time the manxome foe he sought—
So rested he by the Tumtum tree,
And stood awhile in thought.

And as in uffish thought he stood,
The Jabberwock, with eyes of flame,
Came whiffling through the tulgey wood,
And burbled as it came!

One, two! One, two! And through and through
The vorpal blade went snicker-snack!

He left it dead, and with its head
He went galumphing back.

"And hast thou slain the Jabberwock?
Come to my arms, my beamish boy!
O frabjous day! Callooh! Callay!"
He chortled in his joy.

'Twas brillig, and the slithy toves
Did gyre and gimble in the wabe:
All mimsy were the borogoves,
And the mome raths outgrabe.

It's absolutely brilliant, filled with portmanteau words! People
all over the English-speaking world memorize it. There's a
movie by Terry Gilliam based on it, a play, a TV series, a
card game, and endless other cultural references. But what
is it about? A father, a boy with a sword, and the slaying of
the threatening Jubjub bird. The poem's structure is rather
conventional, following the parameters of classic English
poetry. And do you know it's among the most translated
poems in the world as well as the most parodied? There are
approximately sixty different versions of it, in languages as
diverse as Afrikaans, Slovak, and Yiddish. There's even a
version in tlhIngan Hol, the language of the Klingons on
Star Trek. Nonsense makes sense. Even invented words ac-

cumulate layers of meaning and reflect the transformation of society.

VA : They're time capsules.

IS : Imagine a love scene in which all words uttered are in a non-existent language.

VA : It makes me think of the anecdote you mentioned earlier about Edith Piaf and the Pygmies.

IS : The scene takes place whenever people from different cultures fall in love. They might not understand what they say, but they know their passion is authentic. Words need context to have meaning.

VA : You've talked eloquently about our inability to listen to silence. I'm curious about your relationship with music.

IS : In all honesty, I'm envious of musicians. Music has something that literature doesn't: the capacity to generate harmony without emphasizing meaning.

VA : Is music without meaning?

IS : At least in the sense of ideas. Music is about rhythms, not about arguments.

VA : Does music play an important role in your world?

IS : I listen to music all the time—Brahm's Clarinet Quintet in B Minor, Sibelius's Symphonies No. 2 and 7, Chopin's *Études,* Bruch's Violin Concerto No. 1 in G Minor, Mozart's pieces for piano, and almost the entire Bach catalog. Nothing transports me better into another dimension, a state of mindlessness. No internal dialogue occurs in my head, no tangle of ideas. Like

Doctor Faustus, I would give an entire year of my life to be able to create a symphony. I have absolutely no talent for music. My brother got all of it. He apprehends the world through sound.

There is, I suppose, the view that literature is about silence. When we read privately, on our own, we block out the sounds surrounding us. But to me literature generates endless noise. But silence to me conveys visual images. Think of the art of Edward Hopper. In his famous painting *Nighthawks,* made in 1942—while World War II was under way—he depicts a diner (inspired, legend has it, by one in New York City, on Greenwich Avenue) with four lonely characters. The urban landscape is desolate. It's the late hours of the night, it seems. The attendant behind the counter is busy. In the middle is a couple. Are they birds of prey, engaging in an act of flirtation? And who is the fourth character, the suited man sitting in the far left, with his back to us? The street is dark, whereas the diner is filled with fluorescent light, which had just come into use at the time. The scene is framed in such a way that the cafeteria has no entrance, which adds another dimension to Hopper's message of suffocation. Is this what love in the city is about? The painting is about angles: streets, sidewalks, windows, doors . . . Those angles are also to be found in our inner self. Yes, there's a menacing quality to the composition. And sadness, too—sadness and solitude.

VA: What place in the house is connected with silence?

I S : The library, the porch, the garden, wherever one is able to be alone with oneself.

V A : How can we tune in to silence?

I S : On the street, in the park, at home, in the classroom, in the auditorium, in the political forum, and in the concert hall, it's crucial that we sharpen our antennae. The Bible, in Ecclesiastes 20:1–5, states, "To every thing there is a season, and a time to every purpose under the heavens: . . . a time to keep silence, and a time to speak." It adds, "There is the man who keeps quiet and is considered wise; another incurs hatred for talking too much. There is the man who keeps quiet, not knowing how to answer; another keeps quiet, because he knows when to speak. A wise man will keep quiet till the right moment; but a garrulous fool will always misjudge it. The man who talks too much will get himself disliked, and the self-appointed oracle will make himself hated."

Poetry may well be the best tool to appreciate silence. Look at a poem on the page: silence is all around it, in the blank spaces that envelop it. It's also in between the lines and words. Emily Dickinson's poems are small islands of thought encrusted in whiteness, as in the following examples:

Silence is all we dread.
There's Ransom in a Voice—
But Silence is Infinity.
Himself have not a face. (no. 1251)

The words the happy say
Are paltry melody
But those the silent feel
Are beautiful— (no. 1750)

Dickinson was known as "the belle of Amherst." Her home-
stead is three blocks from where I live. In a sense, I came to
New England because of the acquiescence the region symbolizes for me, that nineteenth-century pursuit for the individual's
integration with nature represented in the works of Ralph
Waldo Emerson and Henry David Thoreau. In particular
Thoreau, the New England transcendentalist, was a devotee of
a variety of silence that Dickinson, I'm convinced, wouldn't
have been able to understand. Her attitude was aloof; his was
militant. His solitude was an act of rebellion.

VA : Against what?

IS : Against the mechanization of society that was already palpable
in the mid-nineteenth-century United States, roughly around
the time of the Civil War. In *A Week on the Concord and Merri-
mack Rivers,* Thoreau wrote, "Silence is the universal refuge,
the sequel to all dull discourses and all foolish acts, a balm to
our every chagrin, as welcome after satiety as after disappointment; that background which the painter may not daub, be
he master or bungler, and which, however awkward a figure
we may have made in the foreground, remains ever our invio-
lable asylum, where no indignity can assail, no personality
disturb us." He also suggested that "as the truest society ap-

proaches always nearer to solitude, so the most excellent speech finally falls into Silence. Silence is audible to all men, at all times, in all places. Silence is when we hear inwardly, sound when we hear outwardly. Creation has not displaced her, but is her visible framework and foil. All sounds are her servants, and purveyors, proclaiming not only that their mistress is, but is a rare mistress, and earnestly to be sought after. They are so far akin to Silence that they are but bubbles on her surface."

V A : You mentioned solitude—what is its connection with silence?

I S : Ah, solitude! A balanced relationship, I've learned over the years, emphasizes the interstices of the lovers. Two solitudes come together. Loneliness and solitude aren't synonyms. Solitude is a talent based on balance and self-reliance. It's about discovering the power of nonspeech.

V A : There are several literary classics from Latin America concerned with solitude.

I S : Yes; among them are Octavio Paz's *The Labyrinth of Solitude* and Gabriel García Márquez's *One Hundred Years of Solitude,* published in 1950 and 1963, respectively. The two authors' understanding of solitude is quite different, though. For Paz it's a metaphysical quality; he described Mexicanness as being trapped in introspective, self-generating isolation. Every Mexican lives in it. For García Márquez, solitude is a biblical curse that befalls a single family. Don't you find it ironic that, as populous as our Americas are, characterized by the warmth and accessibility of its people, the concept of solitude should be a defining one? And yet, it's immanent to the region. Wouldn't you say? Isn't the stereotype of the Latin lover that of a solitary figure, a macho always in need of women in order to hide his fear of finding himself alone?

Recently, I've come across the work of Roberto Bolaño, a Chilean writer who died in Barcelona in 2003 at the age of fifty, after a lifetime of disregard for his body—he ate terribly, smoked heavily, and was almost toothless at the end. An astonishing stylist, Bolaño left us, among other books, the novella *A Distant Star,* the collection of stories *Last Nights on Earth,* and the mammoth novel *2006,* which in its Spanish edition has 1,697 pages. To me his characters are more appropriate for describing the Hispanic solitude than anything in Paz and García Márquez.

V A : What is the difference between solitude and loneliness?

I S : Solitude and loneliness—in Spanish, there is only *soledad.* English allows for nuance. What distinguishes the two? Loneliness is an absence. The dictionaries I've visited in search of a definition, including the *OED,* define it negatively, not as a value judgment but following Maimonides' theory of negative attributes: loneliness is the condition of being "without companions," "unfrequented by people," even "desolate."

V A : When discussing music, you talked about mindlessness. In the last chapter of *On Borrowed Words,* you tell of an encounter you had with an amnesiac at the Houston international airport. Every few minutes she would look in her purse for something, an elusive item she desperately needed.

At the end of the anecdote, you offer a meditation on memory and forgetting. Is silence the equivalent of forgetting?

I S : No, forgetting isn't about silence but about incoherence in language. The moment we lose control of our memory, our capacity for speech falters. I find no image more frightening than that of an old person in an asylum, sitting alone, his sight fixed on some empty space, immersed in his own ghosts—and incapable of describing his condition to others. That is my vision of hell.

Shakespeare was infatuated with the impossibility of words. He announces in *Much Ado about Nothing,* "Silence is the perfectest herald of joy: I were but little happy, if I could say how much" (2.1.292–293). Juliet tells Romeo that love cannot be described; and Hamlet learns to recognize, in his journey of ambivalence, that words aren't useful in defining our inner thoughts and motivations. Hamlet's last words in the play, composed in 1599, Shakespeare's *annus mirabilis,* come after his disquisitions on death and disease and are among his most memorable. He asks Horatio to tell Fortinbras "with the occurrents, more and less, which have solicited. The rest is silence" (5.2.357–358).

V A : Hamlet is mad in the end, though.

I S : Aren't we all?

V A : Is there mindlessness in love?

I S : Yes, at the point of orgasm. We enter a state of utter forgetting, in which body and mind become one and speech is reduced to shrieks—or ceases altogether. As Bob Dylan said, "Love is just a four-letter word."

Grateful acknowledgment is made to the copyright holders for permission to reprint the following material:

Anna Akhmatova, "I Wrung My Hands," from *Poems by Akhmatova,* selected, translated, and introduced by Stanley Kunitz and Max Hayward. Boston: Little, Brown, 1973. Used courtesy of Darhansoff, Verrill, Feldman Literary Agents.

Gaius Valerius Catullus, "Carmen 86," from *The Poems of Catullus: A Bilingual Edition,* translated by Peter Green. Berkeley: University of California Press, 2005. Copyright © 2005 Peter Green.

Sor Juana Inés de la Cruz, "Stay, shadow of contentment too short-lived . . . ," from *Poems, Protest, and a Dream* by Sor Juana Inés de la Cruz, translated by Margaret Sayers Peden, with an introduction by Ilan Stavans. New York: Penguin, 1997. Used by permission of the translator.

Ahmed-i Da'î, "The torture of the beloved," from *Ottoman Lyric Poetry: An Anthology,* expanded ed., edited and translated by Walter G. Andrews, Najaat Black, and Mehmet Kalpaklı. Seattle: University of Washington Press, 2006.

Rubén Darío, "Black Dominga," from *Rubén Darío: Selected Writings,* translated by Greg Simon and Steven F. White, with an introduction by Ilan Stavans. New York: Penguin, 2005. Used by permission of the translators.

Bob Dylan, "Love is Just a Four-Letter Word." Copyright © 1967; renewed 1995 Special Rider Music. All rights reserved. International copyright secured. Reprinted by permission.

Moshe ibn Ezra, "Imaginary Eyes," from *The Penguin Book of Hebrew Verse,* edited and translated by T. Carmi. Harmondsworth, Eng.: Penguin, 1981. Copyright © T. Carmi, 1981. Reproduced by permission of Penguin Books Ltd.

Robert Graves, "Symptoms of Love," from *Collected Poems* by Robert Graves. London: Carcaret, 1975.

Wallada bint al-Mustakfi, "Her Right Shoulder," translated by Mona Mikhail. Used by permission of the translator.

Pablo Neruda, "Your Laughter," from *I Explain a Few Things* by Pablo Neruda, edited and translated by Ilan Stavans. New York: Farrar, Straus and Giroux, 2007. Used by permission of the translator.

Francesco Petrarca, "The Voyage," from *The Poetry of Petrarch,* translated and with an introduction by David Young. New York: Farrar, Straus and Giroux, 2004.

INDEX

Thanatos (diety), xvii, 41, 70.
See also Mythology

Eros (Greek word), xiv, 11, 23, 46, 55, 70, 73, 80; and Thanatos (Greek word), xvii, 1, 39, 71, 73, 105

Erotic art, 45–47

Eroticism, xii, xiv, 33, 42; art and, 45–47; Bible and, 54, 57, 58; Foucault and, 29; Hispanic America and, 110–111; Judaism and, 126; Kabbalah and, 62–63; Kama Sutra and, 68; kissing and, 50–51; masturbation and, 169; Octavio Paz on, 93; pornography and, 190; Marquis de Sade and, 32

Essay on Man (Pope), 34

Ethics (Spinoza), 25

Evil, 44, 46, 55, 139, 170, 184

Eyck, Jan van: *Portrait of Giovanni Arnolfini and His Wife*, 38, 78–79

Flaubert, Gustave, 157; *Madame Bovary*, 116

Flavor, 129–130, 132, 146. *See also* Food

Food, 130, 134–135, 146–147; ancient Greece and, 18; Bible and, 148; Christianity and, 147–148;

cinema and, 137–138; "The Disappearance" and, 145; Islam and, 147–148; Judaism and, 147; love and, 130, 132, 147; Roland Barthes on, 131; "Twins" and, 138; words as, 131

Foreplay, 174

Foucault, Michel, 28–30, 32, 37, 167, 171; *The History of Sexuality*, 29

Frank, Jacob, 63, 185

Fray Luis de León. *See* León, Fray Luis de

Freud, Sigmund, xv, 5, 29–33, 70–71, 147, 157, 179; *The Interpretation of Dreams*, 30

Fromm, Erich, 71–72

Gabirol, Solomon (Shlomo) ibn, 22

García Márquez, Gabriel, 244; *Cándida Eréndira*, 154; *Love in the Time of Cholera*, 183; *One Hundred Years of Solitude*, 38, 243

Gardens, 159, 207–210, 241; Eden, 141–142

Ghazals (poetry), 76–77, 207–208

Goethe, Johann Wolfgang von, 128, 129; *The Sorrows of Young Werther*, 127

Golden Ass, The. See *Metamorphoses*

27; *Richard the Second,* 102, 198; *Romeo and Juliet,* 4, 27, 102–104, 245; *Sonnets,* 100–101; *Twelfth Night,* 144

Shame, 2, 44, 54. *See also* Guilt

Shopping malls, 211, 214, 216–219, 223. *See also* Arcades

Silence, 218, 222, 235, 239–245. *See also* Noise

Sin: Alexander Pope on, 98; antinomianism and, 63–64; Christianity and, 140; Dante and, 186; food and, 138; Huguccio on, xv; Judaism and, 143–144, 169–170; Konrad Lorenz on, 145; Lord Byron on, 135; *Malleus Maleficarum* on, 171; OED on, 142; Qur'an on, 148; Saint Augustine on, 143; salvation and, 184; Sir Richard Burton on, 69; in *The Table of the Cardinal Sins* (Bosch), 143; Thomas Aquinas on, 144; in *Twelfth Night* (Shakespeare), 144

Singer, Isaac Bashevis, 118; "A Wedding in Brownsville," 107

Socrates, 18–21, 233

Solitude, 190, 196, 240, 242–245

Sonnets (Shakespeare), 100–101

Sonnets from the Portuguese (Browning), 105–106

Sor Juana Inés de la Cruz. *See* Cruz, Sor Juana Inés de la

Sorrows of Young Werther, The (Goethe), 127

Spanish language usage, ix, 8, 11, 16, 53, 75, 86, 88, 116, 129, 131, 140, 143, 155, 169, 173, 174, 230, 236, 244

Spenser, Edmund: "Epithalamium," 60

Spinoza, Baruch de, xi, xii, 26–27, 206, 207; *Ethics,* 25

Stavans, Ilan: on childhood friendships, 200–206; controversy surrounding Spanglish translation of *Don Quixote,* ix; *Dictionary Days,* xii, xvii, 11, 64, 69, 82, 119, 235; "The Disappearance," 145, 235; on drug usage, 213; on family, 196–197; *The Inveterate Dreamer,* 212; on Jewish upbringing, x, 12–13; on marriage, 80–81; *Octavio Paz: A Meditation,* 28; *On Borrowed Words,* xii, 64, 187, 196, 244; "On Dictionaries: A Conversation with Ilan Stavans," xi; "Otro milagro secreto," 107; *The Oxford Book of Jewish Short Stories,* 31; "Plastic Surgery," 126; *Prontuario,* 106; *The Riddle of Cantinflas,* 70; on